I0814165

THE MYSTERY OF THE TABERNACLE

RABBI KIRT A. SCHNEIDER

The Mystery of the Tabernacle by Rabbi Kirt A. Schneider
Published by Charisma House, an imprint of Charisma Media
1150 Greenwood Blvd., Lake Mary, Florida 32746

All italics in Scripture passages were added to denote emphasis from the author.

Cataloging-in-Publication Data is on file with the Library of Congress.
International Standard Book Number: 978-1-63641-565-9
E-book ISBN: 978-1-63641-566-6

01 2026
Printed in the United States of America

Most Charisma Media products are available at special quantity discounts for bulk purchase for sales promotions, premiums, fund-raising, and educational needs. For details, call us at (407) 333-0600 or visit our website at charismamedia.com.

SPECIAL THANKS

A SPECIAL THANK-YOU TO the pioneering teachers of the Jewish roots of the Christian faith who have gone before me. I owe a debt of gratitude to you.

I want to also express my deep appreciation:

> To my key leaders at Discovering the Jewish Jesus for their love, faith, and support.
>
> To my developmental editor, Adrienne Gaines with Charisma Media, who inspired me to write this book, as well as for her patience, support, and invaluable professional feedback and multidimensional services.
>
> To my beautiful wife, Cynthia Marjorie, for all that she imparts into my life through her love, revelation, and prayers.
>
> To my two beautiful daughters, Alyssa and Summer, for the love, support, joy, and friendship they bring into my life.

And it goes without saying that none of this would have been possible without my God and Savior.

CONTENTS

PART III
THE PRIESTHOOD OF BELIEVERS

Introduction

A GOD WHO COMES CLOSE

OVER THE YEARS, I have taught on the Tabernacle, called the *Mishkan* in Hebrew, many times. And while I've spoken about it before, I believe the Lord inspired me to write this book to bless many more of His children by revealing the spiritual realities and mysteries hidden within the Tabernacle and its furnishings.

Beloved, the Tabernacle is not just ancient history. It is, as the Book of Hebrews tells us, a copy and shadow of heavenly things (Heb. 9:23–24). Every piece of furniture, every sacrifice, every detail of the priestly garments—it all points to Messiah Jesus. As we explore the Tabernacle together, you're going to see how He fulfills every function and how these truths apply directly to your life right now.

When God told Moses, "Let them construct a sanctuary for Me, that I may dwell among them" (Exod. 25:8), it wasn't because He needed a tent. He created the heavens and the earth! No, it was because Father's desire has always been to be close to His people. That hasn't changed. The Tabernacle, the Mishkan, is the visible expression of God's heart to dwell with us—not far away in the heavens but right in the center of our lives.

Religion says, "Climb higher. Work harder. Try to reach God." But the God of Israel did something completely different—He came down. He made His home among His people in the wilderness. And the same God who filled the Tabernacle with His glory wants to fill your life with His presence today.

In this book we're going to explore the Tabernacle's mysteries in three parts:

- Part 1 will take us on a journey through the Tabernacle itself—first the Outer Court, then the Holy Place, and finally beyond the Veil into the Holy of Holies. Each step reveals a deeper level of intimacy with God and a greater revelation of Yeshua.

- Part 2 will focus on the five primary sacrifices offered in the Tabernacle. These weren't just ancient rituals; they were prophetic shadows showing us how to approach God in worship, repentance, and surrender today.

- Part 3 will look at the garments of the high priest. Even the colors, fabrics, and jewels carry meaning—and they speak to your identity as a priest of the Most High in the new covenant.

To help you visualize these truths, I've included images throughout the book. I also want to invite you to scan the following QR code. When you do, you can join me on a walk through a life-size replica of the Tabernacle I visited in Israel. Seeing it with your own eyes will bring these teachings to life in a powerful way.

To view a life-size replica of the Tabernacle, scan this QR code or visit RabbiSchneiderBooks.com/tabernacle/resources.

This book is not just about learning facts. It's about entering into and encountering the very presence of God. The Tabernacle is a mystery—but it's a mystery God delights in revealing. It's His pattern of love, His pathway into His presence, and His prophetic blueprint for intimacy with Him.

Part I

THE TABERNACLE: A BLUEPRINT FOR INTIMACY

Chapter 1

A DWELLING PLACE FOR GOD

WHAT IF THE Creator of the universe—perfect, holy, and in need of nothing—longed to dwell in you? That's exactly what He revealed to Moses when He said,

> Let them construct a sanctuary for Me, that I may dwell among them. According to all that I am going to show you, as the pattern of the tabernacle and the pattern of all its furniture, just so you shall construct it.
>
> —EXODUS 25:8–9

Why did God want a Tabernacle? Because He desired to be close to His people. And that longing has not changed. Still today, Father God wants to be near us.

Isn't that an awesome thing to consider? The Lord of all wants to fellowship with us. Yeshua said to the people of His day, "How often I wanted to gather your children together, the way a hen gathers her chicks under her wings" (Matt. 23:37). Think about that. God needs nothing, yet He finds pleasure and fulfillment in being in relationship with us. In fact, that's why He created humanity—that He might dwell with us in communion.

Yahweh said, "Let Us make man in Our image,

according to Our likeness" (Gen. 1:26). He did this so we could know Him, be like Him, and relate to Him. He made us in His image so we could have the capacity for the type of intimacy with Him that He desires. So we see that from the beginning, God was longing for closeness, and even before Messiah Yeshua came, He gave us a prophetic blueprint for how we can experience union with Him through the Tabernacle.

In the Book of Exodus, or Shemot in Hebrew, the Lord gave Moses precise instructions for how to build the Tabernacle and its furnishings. God was specific, not simply because He wanted it to look a certain way, but because every part of the Tabernacle has a spiritual application. Each element reveals a mystery—a divine key to dwelling in intimacy with God.

As Hebrews 9:23–24 tells us, the Tabernacle was a copy of heavenly realities and pointed to the work of Messiah Jesus. It foreshadowed the things that need to be in place in our own souls so that the Lord Jesus can dwell within us.

You Can Bring God Joy

Many of us don't realize this, but God gets pleasure from us. When we come to Him in prayer, we usually focus on our needs: our finances, family, or health. We look to the Lord as our source, and we should. But true intimacy with God isn't only about what He can do for us. It's also about the joy He receives when we give our love back to Him.

We read in the Hebrew Bible, which is the Old Testament, that the people of Israel grieved the Holy Spirit (Isa. 63:10). To grieve someone means to hurt them emotionally. That's the power we have. We can affect God's heart. We can bring Him sorrow—or we can bring Him joy when we put Him first in our lives.

God is perfectly whole and complete in Himself. He needs nothing. But somehow, we add to His happiness when we choose to love Him. And conversely, when we reject Him, it brings Him pain.

I remember an experience that helped me understand this more deeply. You may know that I came to faith in Yeshua (Jesus) back in 1978 after He appeared to me in a vision. (I won't go into those details here, but I share my full testimony in my book *Called to Breakthrough*.) At the time I was so hungry for truth that I devoured the New Testament. I had grown up in a Jewish family and attended Hebrew school, but I was never taught much about the Bible. I learned to read Hebrew, recite the prayers, and prepare for my bar mitzvah, but I wasn't introduced to God as someone personal, someone who cared for me or wanted me to know Him.

Of course, everyone's experience in Hebrew school is different, but many other Jewish people I know have said the same. They learned to recite the prayers but weren't introduced to God as a friend or a Father who is there for them all the time. So when Messiah Jesus appeared to me and showed me that He was alive—that He was with me and had a plan for my life—my heart leaped. I started running after Yeshua with everything in me. But in the process I left a lot of my Jewish upbringing behind.

Later, I went to Bible school, but they didn't talk much about the connection between the Old and New Testaments. My professors never showed me how Jesus fulfilled the Jewish feasts or how the Tabernacle foreshadowed His work. I slowly began to live as if I were a Gentile believer, still Jewish by birth but disconnected from that identity in my walk with Messiah.

But God graciously restored this part of my life. He showed me how my Jewish heritage related to my relationship with Yeshua. And He began to put the Old and New Testaments together for me.

To pass this understanding on to my children, I wanted our family to start celebrating the Sabbath and the Jewish holy days more intentionally. At first they resisted. Most of their friends were not Jewish, and they didn't want to feel different by honoring Shabbat (Sabbath) and celebrating the Jewish feasts. Whenever I would bring up something Jewish and try to teach them, I could feel them pulling back, and it grieved me deeply.

I share this with you because I think this is how God must feel when we resist or draw back from Him.

This went on for more than a year. Then one day as I was speaking with them, again trying to help them understand who they were, I felt them closing their hearts. Suddenly, my grief just exploded out of me. I started crying and said, "You're hurting me!" I wasn't trying to guilt them. I was just expressing my heart. When they saw me crying—when they realized they had the power to hurt their daddy—it changed them completely. They began to open their hearts and receive what I wanted to give them.

Now my daughters defend the Jewish roots of the Christian faith and educate their Christian friends on the Jewishness of Jesus. They're proud to embrace who we are as Jewish followers of Jesus, but it took realizing that what they were doing was hurting me.

I think we as believers are often like my children. They thought, "Daddy is big and strong. He makes all the rules and gives all the orders. He's too big to be hurt." But they didn't realize that even though I was their dad and their authority figure, they still had the power to hurt me.

That's the way we are at times. We think of God as so big, and He is. We think of Him as the boss, and He is. But like my kids, we don't realize that as small as we are, we have the power to hurt Him. We see Him as El Shaddai, the Almighty, but we don't realize how sensitive He is. Just as my children grieved me, we can grieve God. This is why the New Testament says, "Do not grieve the Holy Spirit" (Eph. 4:30).

God is not only powerful; He's also personal. The Bible says the angels of heaven rejoice when one sinner repents (Luke 15:10). It brings Father God joy when we draw near to Him. But if we reject His love, ignore His voice, or choose our own way, it grieves and hurts Him.

God Dwells with Those Who Love Him

The Lord longs to dwell with us. This is why He had Moses build the Tabernacle.

The Tabernacle is all about love. God wants to dwell with us, and in the following chapters, we will walk through each aspect of the Tabernacle to discover the pattern—the path—that makes it possible for Him to come close.

Chapter 2

THE ONLY WAY IN: THE GATE

FOR FORTY YEARS in the wilderness, the children of Israel witnessed God's manifest presence hovering over the Tabernacle as a cloud by day and a pillar of fire by night. Inside the Tabernacle, in the Holy of Holies, they could literally see the glory of the Lord emanating from between the cherubim over the Ark of the Covenant.

God is now with us through His Spirit. But before the outpouring of the Holy Spirit on the day of Pentecost, people couldn't just sit in their living rooms and encounter God. Apart from a few kings and prophets, the abiding presence of the Spirit—the Ruach HaKodesh—was not widely available. If someone wanted to meet with God, they had to go to a specific place—and that place was the Tabernacle.

Today, God doesn't require us to go to a physical building. But He still calls us to follow the divine pattern established through the Tabernacle. Every measurement, every piece of furniture, and every detail holds prophetic meaning, revealing how we can have fellowship with Him—beginning with the fence.

THE PURPOSE OF THE FENCE

God directed Moses to build a fence around the Tabernacle that was to be about 150 ft. long, 75 ft. wide, and 7 1/2 ft. tall. And it had just one opening through which people could enter.

> You shall make the court of the tabernacle. On the south side there shall be hangings for the court of fine twisted linen one hundred cubits long for one side; and its pillars shall be twenty, with their twenty sockets of bronze; the hooks of the pillars and their bands shall be of silver. Likewise for the north side in length there shall be hangings one hundred cubits long, and its twenty pillars with their twenty sockets of bronze; the hooks of the pillars and their bands shall be of silver. For the width of the court on the west side shall be hangings of fifty cubits with their ten pillars and their ten sockets. The width of the court on the east side shall be fifty cubits. The hangings for the one side of the gate shall be fifteen cubits with their three pillars and their three sockets. And for the other side shall be hangings of fifteen cubits with their three pillars and their three sockets. For the gate of the court there shall be a screen of twenty cubits, of blue and purple and scarlet material and fine twisted linen, the work of a weaver, with their four pillars and their four sockets.
>
> —Exodus 27:9–16

Remember, every part of the Tabernacle—the Mishkan—has prophetic purpose. None of it came into being without a reason. So why did the Lord instruct that a fence be built?

The fence surrounding the Tabernacle revealed that individuals couldn't just approach God however they wanted. If someone wanted to enter the Tabernacle and draw near to the Lord, they couldn't just wander in. The fence allowed only one way in: through the Gate.

What truth does this point to for us in modern times?

It's this: Many people think they can just wander up to God and have a relationship with Him on their own terms. We live in a culture where countless souls have created their own eclectic form of "spirituality." They claim to be spiritual, but the way they approach the Creator is not the one way through which they can truly enter into the divine presence. Self-styled and New Age religion will not bring one into the presence of the Holy One. We are not permitted to create our own religion or path to spiritual maturity. God has ordained the way in.

Similarly, within the church we see a gospel being preached that does not have the cross central, a false gospel that is more man-centered than God-centered. Paul wrote, "For I determined to know nothing among you except Jesus Christ, and Him crucified" (1 Cor. 2:2). Yeshua said, "Whoever wishes to save his life will lose it; but whoever loses his life for My sake will find it" (Matt. 16:25). Yet many people today think God exists just to bless them, make them successful, and fulfill their destiny. The Lord cares about those things, but the problem with that message is that it's not about God first. It's about us first.

There's nothing wrong with becoming all we can be in the Lord. But when the ancient Israelites came to the Tabernacle, they didn't come to get something—they came to worship a holy God. Instead of using God as a means to some worldly end, we must realize that the Lord is holy, that we need to lose our lives to find Him, and that He is our exceedingly great reward (Gen. 15:1).

Messiah Jesus warned, "Many will come in My name, saying, 'I am the Christ,' and will mislead many" (Matt. 24:5).

We're seeing that today in a gospel that exalts self over the cross. But the true gospel is the way of surrender. It calls us to pick up our cross, deny ourselves, and follow Jesus (Matt. 16:24). The real gospel doesn't just teach us how to be our best selves. It teaches us to die to ourselves so that God's power can manifest through our lives.

It's in dying that we live. We must become like the apostle Paul, who said, "I die daily" and that he wanted to "know Him and the power of His resurrection and the fellowship of His sufferings, being conformed to His death" (1 Cor. 15:31; Phil. 3:10). Like Jesus, who picked up His cross and denied Himself to obey the Father, we must follow this same pattern.

A Wall Too High to See Over

As I mentioned, the fence around the Tabernacle was roughly 75 ft. wide, 150 ft. long, and 7 1/2 ft. tall. Interestingly, archaeologists tell us that in ancient Israel, the average male was between only 5'0" and 5'3". I'm about 5'6", so I guess I'm tall compared with ancient Israelites. When people call me short, I say, "Well, I think I'm just built more in the image of Jesus because the average Jewish person of His day was about 5 ft. tall."

Jokes aside, let's think about that. If the fence was 7 1/2 ft. tall and the average Israelite stood around 5 ft. tall, the fence would have been too tall to see over. Through this scenario, the Lord is revealing that those outside the covenant cannot perceive the glory of God. Without redemption through Yeshua, we are blind to the things of the Spirit. The fence teaches us that sin separates us from Him, and He is inaccessible to those who haven't been redeemed through Messiah Jesus. The fence was designed to keep out that which was on the outside. But God in His mercy made a way in.

Outside of Jesus, we're dead in our transgressions and sins (Eph. 2:1) and unable to perceive the things of God. In fact, the Word of God teaches that the path to salvation and into a relationship with the God of heaven is foolishness to the unredeemed (1 Cor. 2:14).

Those who have ears to hear and to whom God has revealed Himself understand that Jesus is the fulfillment of the Gate in the fence of the Tabernacle. He is the one way into God's presence. Unless we enter through Him, we're like those ancient Israelites who couldn't see what the Lord was doing because they were standing outside the Tabernacle.

Yeshua said, "I am the door; if anyone enters through Me, he will be saved" (John 10:9). Those who try to enter another way are thieves and robbers (John 10:1). The Scriptures also say, "There is no other name under heaven that has been given among men by which we must be saved" (Acts 4:12). Just as there was only one entrance into the Tabernacle, where the visible presence of the Lord dwelled, so there is only one way into the presence of God—through Messiah Jesus.

It doesn't do any good to let people think otherwise. I've been to funerals where the preacher implied that the person who just passed away was in heaven, even though they didn't profess to love God. They never read the Bible, never went to church, and never identified themselves as a Christian. Yet here comes the preacher saying the person is in a better place.

Let's get real. We can't be more concerned about offending people than about standing on the truth of God's Word.

When I preach at funerals where I don't know whether the deceased knew Jesus, I don't say they're in hell. It's not my job to say where they ended up if I don't personally know that they loved Jesus. But I'm not going to say someone who didn't follow the Lord is in heaven just to make people feel good.

It doesn't further the cause of the gospel when everyone knows the person wasn't a lover of Jesus, yet the preacher says he's in heaven. That just encourages others to think they're going to heaven too, even if they don't love and serve Jesus. They may think they're right with God when they're still dead in their sins and in need of redemption.

We do people no favors when we hide the truth. We must lift up Yeshua, not compromise the gospel to keep others comfortable. No one goes to heaven except through Jesus. There was only one entrance into the Tabernacle, one Gate, which pointed to the reality that there is still only one way to Father God today.

Yeshua said to the Jewish people of His day, "Unless you believe that I am He, you will die in your sins" (John 8:24). A life that is not surrendered to Messiah Jesus will not enter the kingdom of God.

The Tabernacle's fence teaches us that not everyone is inside. Let's not compromise the gospel. Let's not be so afraid of hurting people's feelings that we're unwilling to speak the truth. There is only one way in. Let's lift up the name of Yeshua and walk the narrow road that leads to life.

Finally, today we often hear people preach the gospel of salvation, but Yeshua didn't just preach salvation from sin—He preached the gospel of the kingdom. He didn't tell people to say a quick sinner's prayer. He said, "Pick up your cross, deny yourself, and follow Me. He who loses his life for My sake shall find it." Beloved, this is the one doorway in, which the ancient Tabernacle prophetically pointed to.

Chapter 3

THE PLACE OF ATONEMENT: THE BRAZEN ALTAR

When the ancient Israelites entered through the one Gate—the only way in—they stepped into the Outer Court. And the first thing they encountered was the Brazen (brass) Altar. This was the place of sacrifice.

> And you shall make the altar of acacia wood, five cubits long and five cubits wide; the altar shall be square, and its height shall be three cubits. You shall make its horns on its four corners; its horns shall be of one piece with it, and you shall overlay it with bronze.
>
> —Exodus 27:1–2

Here's what would happen: The worshipper would bring with him a clean, unblemished (kosher) animal. Then, under the instruction of the priests at the altar, the worshipper would place his hands on the head of the animal. But he didn't just touch it lightly. The Hebrew word *sāmaḵ*, translated "put" in Leviticus 1:4, indicates that he didn't just lay his hands gently on the animal's head. Rather, the word carries the idea of pressing into it.

The worshipper leaned into the sacrifice, pressing his weight into the animal's head. In doing so, he symbolically transferred his sin into the innocent creature. That animal would then be slaughtered and its blood smeared around the altar. It died in the worshipper's place, and God would not hold the person's sin against him.

Hebrews 9 tells us this entire process was a copy—a shadow—of the ultimate sacrifice: Messiah Jesus. The blood of bulls and goats could never truly take away sin, but God accepted it as a temporary covering until Jesus came. When Yeshua gave His life on the cross, our sin was transferred into Him just as the ancient worshipper's sin was symbolically transferred to the animal sacrifice.

Scripture confirms this in 1 Peter 2:24: "He Himself bore our sins in His body on the cross, so that we might die to sin and live to righteousness." Just as the worshipper leaned his full weight into the animal, the full weight of our sin was placed on Yeshua. And He—the innocent—died in the place of the guilty.

Because of what Jesus did, God now looks at you and me as holy and blameless. Why? Because the sin is not in us anymore. It was transferred. It was judged. It was dealt with—in Yeshua.

That's why you can look in the mirror and say, "I'm holy and blameless before God," according to Ephesians 1–2. You might ask, "How can I say that when I just lost my temper or was careless with my words?" The answer is, your forgiveness isn't based on your performance; it's based on the finished work of Jesus, who took all your sins—past, present, and future—into His body and paid the penalty once and for all.

Now, if the blood of bulls and goats can't take away our sin, what was happening spiritually during those ancient animal sacrifices? Consider this illustration. When you go to the store and swipe your credit card, the merchant gives you the merchandise even though no physical money changed hands. Why? Because the merchant knows the real payment is coming.

That's what those animal sacrifices were like. They were the credit card. The worshipper's sin wasn't truly removed yet, but the Lord accepted the offering because He knew the real payment was coming—Messiah Yeshua.

As we've seen, the Tabernacle is a copy of heavenly things, and Yeshua is the fulfillment. The Tabernacle was built so that the Lord could dwell with His people, but now God has given us His Son, Emmanuel—God with us. Jesus is the way through which we have fellowship with God. The entire Tabernacle points to Him, and the altar of sacrifice is where it all begins.

First Things First

The prophetic blueprint within the Tabernacle shows us that if we want to have fellowship with God, our sin needs to be atoned for. That's why when the ancient worshipper entered the Tabernacle, the first thing he encountered was the Brazen Altar.

Beloved, you cannot come close to God without first having your sin dealt with. Sin separates us from a holy God, and the only way to be brought back into communion with Him is to deal with that sin problem. The Bible tells us, "The soul who sins shall die" (Ezek. 18:20, NKJV). That means the penalty for sin—even just one sin—is death.

But God made a way. His remedy is substitution—that an

innocent one would die in place of the guilty. This is why blood is such a prominent theme in the Scriptures.

At the first Passover, the Israelites put the blood of the lamb on the doorposts of their homes. When the angel of death passed through Egypt to strike down every firstborn, he passed over that home if he saw the blood. The blood allowed them to escape judgment.

Later, at Mount Sinai, after Moses read the Laws of the Torah God had given, the people responded by saying, "All the words which the Lord has spoken we will do!" (Exod. 24:3). As soon as they accepted the covenant, Moses sprinkled them with blood. Why? Because they couldn't come into relationship with Yahweh without sacrificial atonement. Their sin had to be addressed before they could walk in fellowship with Him.

The Torah tells us in the Book of Leviticus, or Vayikra in Hebrew, "For the life of the flesh is in the blood, and I have given it to you on the altar to make atonement for your souls; for it is the blood by reason of the life that makes atonement" (Lev. 17:11). This is why Yeshua had to die and why the soldiers pierced His side at the crucifixion. His blood being poured out symbolized that His life had been given. An innocent one died so we, the guilty, could go free.

This same truth is seen in what is considered the highest holy day of the Jewish year, Yom Kippur, the Day of Atonement. In ancient times the high priests would go into the Holy of Holies with the blood of bulls and goats and pour it on top of the Ark of the Covenant, where the Ten Commandments were housed. In doing this, the priest covered Israel's sin against God's holy Law.

Our Greatest Need

So let me ask you this: Do you understand your greatest need? It's not happiness. It's not wealth. It's not even physical health. Your greatest need is to have your sins atoned for. This, again, is why in the pattern of the Tabernacle the first thing we encounter is the Brazen Altar. It shows that if we want to have a relationship with God, we must first deal with our sin.

It doesn't matter how many good deeds you've done. You can be respected by your friends, neighbors, coworkers, and the rest of the world. But unless your sins are washed away because you accepted the gift God gave you when He sent His Son to die for your sins, you will stand guilty before God.

Remember, the Bible says the soul that sins shall die (Ezek. 18:20). But Jesus loves us so much that He died in our place. When we accept His gift, our sins are blotted out, we receive the Holy Spirit, and we gain eternal life. This is why, as we saw in the last chapter, there is only one door—one Gate—into the Tabernacle. It represents Jesus, the only way to eternal life.

Maybe you've been listening to a false gospel, one that says Jesus died to make you rich or to fulfill your dreams. But Jesus didn't die to make us somebody in this world. He died because we were wretched sinners who needed forgiveness. And outside of God's mercy, we would be destined to outer darkness and separation from God forever.

If you've never truly received Him—never said, "Yeshua, I need You to wash my sins away"—then I invite you to pray with me right now:

Lord Jesus, I realize that when You died on the cross, it was for me, and the way for me not to be judged by Father God is to accept You and what You did for me by dying in my place. I thank You right now, Jesus, that You took my sin in Your body and washed it away. I receive Your love and forgiveness, and I want to live the rest of my life following You the way You've asked me to. I want to learn how to pick up my cross, denying my own will and the desires of my flesh, and to follow You. I give You my heart this day, Jesus. Come live inside me forever and sanctify me in Your truth. Amen.

Friend, without forgiveness for our sin, there is no fellowship with God. But because of what Yeshua did, God can forgive us. Yet when we talk about forgiveness, we're not talking about God saying, "It's OK; what you did wasn't that bad." He forgives us because justice has been satisfied. The punishment has been paid—it fell on Jesus.

"He made Him who knew no sin to be sin on our behalf, so that we might become the righteousness of God in Him" (2 Cor. 5:21). Jesus was beaten, whipped, spit on, and scourged. His side was pierced. And then the Father turned away from Him, causing Him to cry out, "My God, My God, why have You forsaken me?" (See Matthew 27:46.)

He experienced the separation from God that you and I should have endured. He descended into the lower parts of the earth (Eph. 4:9), which I believe refers to hell, and faced the torment we deserved. Then God raised Him from the dead and seated Him at His right hand, where He sits now, making intercession for us as our Savior.

God is able to forgive us today because the penalty for our sin has been paid by Jesus.

Likewise, when we forgive others, it's not because what the person did wasn't that bad. We forgive because Jesus died for them too. Their sin, like ours, was already punished at the cross. We can forgive for the same reason God can forgive—because His justice has been satisfied.

This is important for us to understand. When we forgive others, we're not saying the person didn't cause us pain. We're saying, "I forgive you because Jesus died for your sins, just as He died for mine. I forgive because He forgave me, and He commands me to do the same."

Beloved, this is the gospel. This is the message of the Brazen Altar. The only way in is through Yeshua. And when we enter through that one gate, we come face-to-face with the altar: the place of sacrifice. That's the starting point of true relationship with God—accepting the gift Yeshua gave us when He, the innocent One, became the ultimate sacrifice for our sins, dying in our place so we, the guilty, could go free.

Chapter 4

CLEANSED FOR INTIMACY: THE BRASS LAVER

As we continue to move through the Outer Court toward the Holy Place in the Tabernacle, once we pass the Brazen Altar, the next piece of furniture we encounter is the Brass Laver.

> The Lord spoke to Moses, saying, "You shall also make a laver of bronze, with its base of bronze, for washing; and you shall put it between the tent of meeting and the altar, and you shall put water in it. Aaron and his sons shall wash their hands and their feet from it; when they enter the tent of meeting, they shall wash with water, so that they will not die; or when they approach the altar to minister, by offering up in smoke a fire sacrifice to the Lord. So they shall wash their hands and their feet, so that they will not die; and it shall be a perpetual statute for them, for Aaron and his descendants throughout their generations."
>
> —Exodus 30:17–21

Like all the other elements in the Tabernacle, the Lord gave specific instructions not only for how the laver should be used but also for how it should be constructed. Exodus 38:8 tells us, "Moreover, he made the laver of bronze with its base of bronze, from the mirrors of the serving women who served at the doorway of the tent of meeting." This is one of my favorite verses in the Bible about the Brass Laver. The

Lord told Moses that the Brass Laver had to come from the mirrors outside the doorway of the Tabernacle.

When God gave instructions for building something, He would typically specify what kind of material to use (gold, silver, acacia wood, and so on) or the color (blue, purple, or scarlet). But rarely did He say exactly where the material should come from. Yet in this particular case, the Lord was very specific. The brass was to come from the mirrors of the women who ministered outside the Tabernacle.

Remember, the Tabernacle is a pattern of heavenly things. Every piece of furniture, every dimension, the way everything was laid out—it all has application to our lives as followers of Jesus. There's meaning in every aspect of the Tabernacle, including the requirement that the brass in the laver be made from mirrors. But before we dive into why God was so specific about that, let's first explore what the Brass Laver was.

The Brass Laver was a basin filled with water, where the priests would go each day to wash themselves before entering the Tabernacle. Their sins were legally forgiven at the Brazen Altar. But the effects of living in a sinful world and being human still left them with the stain of sin.

The same is true of us. Just because we're legally forgiven of our sins doesn't mean we don't still need to be cleansed daily. That's what the Bible tells us. Our sins are forgiven, yet 1 John 1:9 also says, "If we confess our sins, He is faithful and righteous to forgive us our sins and to cleanse us from all unrighteousness." Like the ancient priests who received legal forgiveness at the Brazen Altar but still needed an experiential cleansing at the Brass Laver, we who follow Yeshua have been forgiven of the sins we've committed, but we still must be cleansed from the effects of those sins.

We live in a world filled with sin, and like those ancient priests, we must be cleansed every day of the filth and pollution we pick up—not only from the world around us but also from what is hidden in our own hearts. This is why the priest had to go to the Brass Laver every day.

A Mirror for the Soul

As we've seen, the Brass Laver was made from the mirrors of the women who ministered outside the Tabernacle. Why would God require that the brass come from mirrors? Consider what a mirror is used for: to look at oneself. You don't use a mirror to see what someone else looks like. You use it to see your own reflection.

The laver had to be made from mirrors because God wants us to examine our lives through the gaze of the Holy Spirit. That's the principle revealed through the Brass Laver. I believe the Lord was saying to us prophetically that He wants us to allow Him to hold a mirror up to our lives—to show us who we are—and then invite us to agree with Him about what He reveals. When we do, we can confess our sin rather than try to justify ourselves, make excuses, or hide from our guilt.

A lot of times, people get trapped in judging other people. But Jesus said, Take the log out of your own eye before you try to take the speck out of somebody else's (Matt. 7:3–5). Too often people hear a sermon that directly applies to their life, yet all they can think of is how it relates to someone else:

their brother-in-law, their mom, their neighbor, or so-and-so at work. They can't see that the sermon is meant for them.

This is why we must look at our own lives through the lens of the Holy Spirit. Each day, the priest would go in to the Brass Laver, and as he leaned over it in that extreme desert sun and looked into the water, he saw a reflection of himself. Similarly, God is saying to you and me, "If you want to enter into deep, abiding fellowship with Me, you need to look at yourself. Allow Me to show you who you are in My eyes and agree with Me about what I reveal."

One thing I've learned is that when we are confronted with truth, we're going to react one of two ways. Either we defend ourselves and point our finger at everyone else, or we say, "Yes, that's true. Forgive me, Lord. Cleanse me." When someone holds a mirror up to our face and points out an issue we have, we have a choice. And if we want to be cleansed, we must agree with the Holy Spirit, saying, "Yes, Lord, You're right. I'm guilty. Forgive me." We must come to the Lord in humility like the tax collector in Luke 18:13, who beat his hands against his chest and cried, "God, be merciful to me, the sinner!" Yeshua said that man went home justified.

When the Lord holds that mirror to our faces and talks to us about the way we spoke to our family or how we mishandled a situation at work, will we allow ourselves to say, "Yes, Lord, forgive me; I was wrong"? Or are we going to say, "I only responded that way because of what so-and-so did"? Are we going to make our excuses and judge other people, or are we going to accept responsibility for our own sin at the Brass Laver—the mirror of the Holy Spirit—and say, "God,

I'm guilty; please cleanse me, change me, and make me whole"?

True intimacy with God can only be achieved when we humble ourselves, allow the Holy Spirit to hold His mirror up to our faces, and agree with what He reveals.

The Lord Wants to Go Deeper

Several years ago the Lord spoke to me in a dream that has stuck with me. I was ministering at a congregation I once pastored, and as I was preaching, everyone suddenly stood up and started reciting the Pledge of Allegiance. It was so loud that it drowned out my message. Humiliated, I left the pulpit and hid in the restroom.

I said, "Lord, I feel so embarrassed. What should I do?" He answered, "Go back in there and finish." I did not want to, but I obeyed. As I walked behind the pulpit, somebody yelled out, "They don't want to listen to you anymore!" But I finished the message, and the dream ended.

I was grieved and confused. I thought, "Lord, what did I do? Where have I failed as a leader that the congregation would rise up like that in the middle of my message and show such disrespect? Where am I weak? What vulnerability or insecurity am I showing that people would do that to me while I'm preaching Your Word?"

Several days later the Holy Spirit clearly communicated to my heart: "It wasn't you. It wasn't your weakness as a leader that made them rise up and drown out your preaching with the Pledge of Allegiance. I was showing you that people aren't being cleansed by My Word. They're more concerned about becoming successful and achieving the American dream than they are about following Me, allowing Me to cleanse them, and letting Me become preeminent in their lives."

The Lord is saying to us today, "Unless My people are waking up every day and asking Me to cleanse them of the worldly mindset they've picked up, unless they're looking honestly at themselves and saying, 'Lord, You're right; this is true about me,' they won't experience true intimacy with Me."

If we'll allow the Holy Spirit to hold the mirror up to our lives, agree with what He reveals, and repent, He will change us. When we confess our faults, God is faithful and just to forgive our sins and cleanse us of all unrighteousness (1 John 1:9). If we respond to His correction with humility and honesty, He will purify us and bring us into true relationship with Him.

You see, we talk a lot today about having a relationship with God, but a relationship with God comes to pass through obedience. That's the key. It's more than just saying a sinner's prayer. Yes, it's essential to ask the Lord to forgive us and come into our lives, but that's only the entry point. If we want to walk in relationship with Him, we must come under obedience.

That's why Jesus said in John 14:21 and 23, "He who has My commandments and keeps them is the one who loves Me; and he who loves Me will be loved by My Father, and I will love him and will disclose Myself to him....If anyone loves Me, he will keep My word; and My Father will love him, and We will come to him and make Our abode with him." The path to intimacy with God isn't just forgiveness; it's transformation. And transformation begins at the Brass Laver, where the Holy Spirit washes us with truth.

Chapter 5

THE FLAME OF THE SPIRIT: THE GOLDEN MENORAH

As we have seen, the Tabernacle was crafted according to the pattern Yahweh gave Moses on Mount Sinai. Each item carries prophetic significance and was divinely positioned to teach us how to progress in intimacy with Him.

We start at the altar, where our sins are forgiven, and then we move to the Brass Laver, where we become experientially sanctified as the Lord shows us ourselves and we ask Him to cleanse us. Once that happens, we progress from the Outer Court and enter the Tabernacle itself. There we find two rooms: the Holy Place and the Holy of Holies, where the presence of the Lord dwelled.

The Holy Place was approximately 30 ft. long, 15 ft. wide, and 15 ft. tall, and the first item we would encounter there was the Golden Menorah.

> Then you shall make a lampstand of pure gold. The lampstand and its base and its shaft are to be made of hammered work; its cups, its bulbs and its flowers shall be of one piece with it....See that you make them after the pattern for them, which was shown to you on the mountain.
>
> —Exodus 25:31, 40

The Golden Menorah, also called the Golden Lampstand, was *made from one pure piece of gold that had been hammered into shape*. It wasn't piecemealed together. The menorah had been molded to form one unified piece with *seven branches*, or candlesticks, with flames emanating from each one. The number seven represents perfection, fullness, and completion.

I believe these seven flames are a prophetic shadow of the Holy Spirit, or in Hebrew, the Ruach HaKodesh. We see this in Revelation 1, when the Spirit of God came upon John during his exile on the island of Patmos. While John was caught up in the Spirit, he was greeted by Yeshua, who said:

> Grace to you and peace, from Him who is and who was and who is to come, and from the *seven Spirits who are before His throne.*
>
> —Revelation 1:4

There's only one person who is, who was, and who is to come—the eternal God. So God is greeting John and saying, "I'm the eternal One. I'm the One who is, was, and is to come, and I'm the One with the seven Spirits of God proceeding from My throne."

These aren't seven individual spirits. There is only one Holy Spirit, just as the menorah had seven flames but was only one lampstand.

We see this idea reinforced in Revelation 3:1: "To the angel of the church in Sardis write: He who has the seven Spirits of God and the seven stars, says this…"

Hebrews 9 teaches that the Tabernacle is a shadow—a copy—of Yeshua. The Golden Menorah inside the Tabernacle, represents Messiah Jesus and the Spirit that proceeds from Him.

Through the Golden Lampstand, we understand that if

we're going to walk with God, we must relate to Him through His Spirit. Romans 8:14 (NKJV) tells us, "As many as are led by the Spirit of God, these are sons of God."

Some of us may be sincere lovers of God's Word but are not in touch with the Holy Spirit. Some in the church have been taught that when the Bible was written, the gifts of the Spirit ceased. This type of teaching desensitizes people to the presence of the Holy Spirit and His ever-present communication to us. There is a mystery in being led by the Lord, and it involves Him supernaturally guiding us by His Spirit.

Let me tell you, Father God cares about all the details of your life, but when you're in the market for a house or looking to get married, the Bible isn't going to tell you which house to buy or the name of the person you're supposed to marry. God sent His Spirit to lead you in making those decisions. But unless we develop a sensitivity to the Holy Spirit, we're going to miss His direction. We must have ears that are open to hear what the Spirit is saying.

A Speaking Spirit

In Acts 2, when the Spirit of God was poured out on the day of Pentecost, "tongues as of fire" appeared and rested on each believer, and "they were all filled with the Holy Spirit and began to speak with other tongues, as the Spirit was giving them utterance" (vv. 3–4).

The tongues spoken that day were not the unknown prayer language often emphasized in Pentecostal circles. I'm not putting that down. I speak in tongues myself. But I want to bring some biblical clarity. The tongues spoken in Acts

2 were known languages. The believers were supernaturally empowered to proclaim the gospel in languages they had never learned. It would be like me suddenly proclaiming the gospel in fluent Japanese, though I've never studied it.

Every gift that God gives is good, and I believe it's a blessing to speak in that type of tongues. But when the Holy Spirit appeared to the believers as tongues of fire, the emphasis wasn't on their need to speak in an unknown prayer language but on the fact that God had come, was alive, and was speaking. That's why the Spirit appeared as tongues of fire.

That means God is now speaking to His children. Yeshua said of Himself, "My sheep hear My voice, and I know them, and they follow Me" (John 10:27). We need to realize that God is alive, and He's speaking to us today.

In fact, God's Spirit fell so powerfully on the day of Pentecost that some people thought the believers were drunk. But Peter stood up and declared:

> These men are not drunk, as you suppose, for it is only the third hour of the day; but this is what was spoken of through the prophet Joel: "And it shall be in the last days," God says, "that I will pour forth of My Spirit on all mankind; and your sons and your daughters shall prophesy, and your young men shall see visions, and your old men shall dream dreams."
>
> —Acts 2:15–17

What had taken place in that upper room was this event Joel had prophesied about: God's Spirit being poured out. He came to us speaking, and now all flesh—not just a select few but all classes of people—would be able to speak by inspiration of the Holy Spirit. They would be able to prophesy, see in the Spirit, and have dreams at night from the Holy Spirit.

God's Spirit speaks through prophecy

Joel said, "Your sons and your daughters shall prophesy." To prophesy simply means to speak by inspiration of the Spirit. You don't have to say "Thus saith the Lord" to prophesy. You just have to be led of the Spirit. If you're advising your child and God is giving you wisdom for that counsel, you're prophesying. You're speaking by inspiration of the Spirit.

God's Spirit speaks through visions

Joel's prophecy went on to say, "Your young men shall see visions." You may think, "I've never seen a vision." But if you are a child of God, He wants to speak to you in visions. All visions aren't epic like the one John had in the Book of Revelation or the one the prophet had in Isaiah 6. The visions that should be common for all of us today are when God speaks by putting images in our minds. Those pictures often speak a thousand words.

This has happened to me several times. Years ago I was talking with a man in my congregation, and all of a sudden I saw something like an axe coming down over his head. It was so subtle that I would have missed it had I not been paying attention. I said to him, "I just saw this picture in my mind: an axe above your head. Is anything going on?" He replied, "I just found out I'm getting sued." This is how the Holy Spirit often uses visions today. He will put pictures in our minds that communicate a thousand words that will lead us in life.

Another example comes to mind. I was thinking of getting

involved in a specific endeavor, and I was sitting before the Lord one day, asking Him whether I should take part. As I was sitting before the Lord, a picture appeared in my mind of what looked like a knee joint: the ball and socket. I don't think I've ever thought about or pictured a joint in my life, but suddenly as I'm thinking about getting involved in this venture, a joint appears in my mind, the ball fitting right into the socket. The Lord was telling me, "This is right for you. It fits you perfectly. I want you to get involved in this right now."

God's Spirit speaks through dreams

Finally, Joel said, "Your old men shall dream dreams." These aren't necessarily dreams of accomplishing something great. He's talking about God speaking to us in our sleep.

Dreams are one of the most common vehicles of revelation we find in Scripture. Joseph was led by dreams (Gen. 37:5–10, chapters 40–41). Jacob saw the Lord's angels ascending and descending from heaven when he laid his head on the rock at Bethel. As a result, he realized that God was with him (Gen. 28:10–17). Paul went into a night trance and realized he was supposed to preach the gospel in Macedonia (Acts 16:9–10). Similarly, Yeshua's earthly father, Joseph, was led by a dream to take baby Jesus to Egypt. Then after the ruler of Israel had died, ending the danger to the male Hebrew children, the angel spoke to Joseph in a dream again, telling him to take Yeshua back to Israel (Matt. 2:13, 19–21).

God is not sleeping when we're sleeping. Often He is leading us. Many times when we're asleep, we're not as tied to the material world as when we're awake. When we're kind of hovering between the natural and the spiritual realms, God intrudes into our minds and speaks to us. This is why we need to pay attention to our dreams. I can't tell you all the times God has stopped me from making a wrong decision through a dream.

Expect God to Lead You

Beloved, if we want to walk in intimacy with God, we must realize that God is a living Being who is still speaking to us by His Spirit. If you're not expecting Him to speak to you, you're probably not going to hear Him when He does because, as the prophet Elijah discovered, sometimes He's not in the fire. He's not in the earthquake. He's in the still small voice (1 Kings 19:11–13). There have been many times when the Lord has spoken to me so subtly that if I'd not been paying attention, I would not have recognized His voice.

In 1 Samuel 3, a young Samuel was in bed, and the Lord kept coming to him. He thought someone else was speaking to him until the priest Eli informed him that he was hearing the Lord's voice. We too need to be aware that God is speaking to us, or we're going to miss His voice.

Yeshua said, "He who believes in Me, as the Scripture said, 'From his innermost being will flow rivers of living water'" (John 7:38). He was speaking of His Spirit.

Remember Yeshua's discussion with the Samaritan woman at the well? They began to dialogue about spiritual things, and she said, "You're a Jewish person. You worship in Jerusalem. But we Samaritans worship over on that mountain." And Yeshua said:

> But an hour is coming, and now is, when the true worshipers will worship the Father in spirit and truth; for such people the Father seeks to be His worshipers. God is spirit, and those who worship him must worship in spirit and truth.
>
> —John 4:23–24

If we're going to truly worship God, it's not going to be by our intellect alone. God is Spirit, and the way we relate to Him is through spirit. The Bible tells us that God's Spirit has been given to us that we might freely know the things of God (1 Cor. 2:12). But especially in the Western world, we have been so trained by the culture to live in the realm of intellectualism and logic that we're not being led by the Spirit of God. His ways are not our ways, and His thoughts are not our thoughts. If we want to know Him, we must become attuned to His Spirit.

The Bible says we are not to lean on our own understanding, but in all our ways acknowledge Him, and He'll direct our path (Prov. 3:5–6). I want you to know, if I relied on my own reason and logic, I would not be where I am today. In fact, I wouldn't even believe in Messiah Jesus because all the people around me—the whole Jewish community I grew up within—told me I was a heretic for believing in Yeshua.

Too many believers are trapped in a religion that's devoid of power, just as the apostle Paul said (2 Tim. 3:5). They've been taught that all there is to the Christian life is knowing the Bible. Studying the Scriptures is the foundation of our walk with Yeshua, but the written Word is not designed to replace the living Word—Yeshua (John 1:1). It's designed to lead us to Him.

Yeshua's first disciples didn't have Bibles like we do today. Some of Paul's letters were eventually floating around among the churches, but the first- and second-century believers didn't have leather-bound copies of the Scriptures with tabs to help them find the various books. They were led by God's Spirit. Messiah Jesus said in John 14, "I'm going away, but I'm not going to leave you as orphans. I'm going to send you the Comforter, the Ruach HaKodesh, the Holy Spirit, and He will lead you into all truth and remind you of all that I have said to you." (See John 14:16–18, 26.)

Paul, Peter, Timothy—they were all led by the Spirit of God, and we must be too. We don't have to fear being misled if we follow the Holy Spirit. We can trust that the Spirit of God will never contradict the written Word of God—because the Spirit of God is the author of the written Word of God.

> Now suppose one of you fathers is asked by his son for a fish; he will not give him a snake instead of a fish, will he?...If you then, being evil, know how to give good gifts to your children, how much more will your heavenly Father give the Holy Spirit to those who ask Him?
>
> —Luke 11:11, 13

Revelation Comes by the Spirit

Many people hear the Word of God with their ears, and even though they might mentally agree with it, they still are not brought into the fullness of the truth. This is because you can't receive the Word just with your intellect. The Word has to be imparted to you as a revelation by the Spirit. This is what was happening in John 6:41–45 when the Jewish religious leaders could not receive Yeshua's word:

> Therefore the Jews were grumbling about Him, because He said, "I am the bread that came down out of heaven." They were saying, "Is not this Jesus, the son of Joseph, whose father and mother we know? How does He now say, 'I have come down out of heaven'?" Jesus answered and said to them, "Do not grumble among yourselves. No one can come to Me unless the Father who sent Me draws him; and I will raise him up on the last day. It is written in the prophets, 'And they shall all be taught of God.' Everyone who has heard and learned from the Father, comes to Me."

Everyone who receives revelation—everyone who receives the divine light of the Holy Spirit, symbolized by the menorah in the Tabernacle—will respond to God's Word.

This is likewise illustrated when Yeshua asked His disciples, "Who do people say I am?"

> And they said, "Some say John the Baptist; and others, Elijah; but still others, Jeremiah, or one of the prophets." He said to them, "But who do you say that I am?" Simon Peter answered, "You are the Christ, the Son of the living God." And Jesus said to him, "Blessed are you, Simon Barjona, because flesh and blood did not *reveal this to you*, but My Father who is in heaven."
>
> —Matthew 16:13–17

It's so important to recognize how dependent we are upon the Ruach HaKodesh, who gives true inner revelation. You can only know the truth of God's Word in your spirit man through revelation. You might think you know it because you understand it with your head, but you don't really get it until it's revealed deep in your spirit.

Years ago I had been ministering at a church and brought our dance team. It was a bitterly cold winter night, and as we were walking out of the church, one of the dance team members fell on the icy pavement and hurt herself. I asked the Lord, "Why did this happen? You could have prevented her from falling in that frigid parking lot. Why didn't You do that?" So many times I saw people who were professing the name of Jesus but falling and failing in life. I said, "Lord, unless You give me the answer to this, I won't be able to move forward with You the way I need to."

Several days later, as I was driving, I sensed the Holy Spirit say, "The reason you're seeing My people falling is because they're not trusting Me." But when He said that, I didn't hear it just with my ears. It came with a deep revelation in my spirit. The Spirit of God imparted to my inner man an understanding of what He meant. And what He was saying was, "They're not clinging to Me as their source for life. They're just running ahead of Me, relying on their own flesh."

That set me free because I understood that the reason so many who profess Jesus as their Lord live in a constant cycle of defeat rather than abundance wasn't because God couldn't be trusted; it was because they weren't fully depending on Him and being strengthened by His Spirit as a result.

We need to become more dependent on the Ruach HaKodesh, the Holy Spirit. We need to get back to the mystical element of the faith and spend time just sitting before the Lord waiting on Him, knowing, as Paul said, that the mystery of the gospel is Messiah in us, the hope of glory

(Col. 1:27). The Bible tells us, "Do you not know that you are a temple of God and that the Spirit of God dwells in you?" (1 Cor. 3:16). We have a life force within us. We've been made partakers of the divine nature, and we need to stop relying on false comforts, distractions, and even other people and start relying on Father God, on Messiah, and on the Ruach HaKodesh as our source.

Illuminated by the Spirit

It's so easy to be deceived in life. The only way we'll be able to think clearly is through the light the Holy Spirit gives us. How often do conflicts develop in relationships because we're perceiving each other wrongly? The enemy is making us feel insulted by the way someone looked at us or talked to us. We interpret it one way when, in reality, something completely different was happening. We thought they were snubbing us, but they actually were just afraid.

These kinds of wrong perceptions can develop when our minds are not illuminated by the Holy Spirit. David said in Psalm 36:9, "For with You is the fountain of life; in Your light we see light." That light is the Holy Spirit—the light of the Golden Menorah. If we want to really see, if we truly want to understand, we need our lives to be illuminated by the Holy Spirit. To do that, we must learn to honor Him more, depend on Him more, and stop relying on the world's counsel. A lot of the "wisdom" within Christendom today is not really godly. Oftentimes it's just worldly counsel wrapped in spiritual-sounding packaging.

So I want to encourage you to honor the Ruach HaKodesh.

Give Him more time. Sit before Him every day and say, "Holy Spirit, I bless You. I submit myself to You today. Train me in Your ways. Help me to stop relying on my friends too much for advice and instead look to Your Spirit to teach me, strengthen me, gird me, and guide me through life."

Only when we stop depending on man and start relying on God and His Spirit will we be victors. "'Not by might nor by power, but by My Spirit,' says the LORD of hosts" (Zech. 4:6). When Israel relied on God, they were victorious in war. But when they began to look at their enemies instead of the Lord, they would say, "These enemies are powerful, so let's make alliances with other armies. That way we'll have enough manpower to defeat our enemies." Yet instead of winning, they started losing the battle.

"Thus says the LORD, 'Cursed is the man who trusts in mankind and makes flesh his strength, and whose heart turns away from the LORD'" (Jer. 17:5). Many of us today are being defeated in life because we're making alliances with the world. We're relying on the world to overcome, and it's going to do for us the same thing it did to Israel—bring us to defeat. God wants us to get back to the simplicity of the gospel, and that is through relying on His Spirit to lead us into all truth (John 16:7).

Beloved, the Holy Spirit, represented by the Golden Menorah, is the Spirit of truth. He is not an optional accessory to the Christian life—He is the power source. As the menorah lit the Tabernacle, so the Spirit illuminates our lives. Without Him, we walk in darkness. But when we give Him preeminence in our lives and allow Him to lead us, He will set us free in Yeshua's name, and we will walk in the light of truth and victory.

Chapter 6

LIVING IN GOD'S LOVE: THE TABLE OF SHOWBREAD

THE LORD TOLD Moses to construct the Tabernacle so that He might dwell among His people (Exod. 25:8). When you think about it, the Tabernacle was a manifestation of God's love. He wanted to be near His people, to dwell in their midst. In that sense you could call it the Tabernacle of love because it reveals God's desire to relate to us and how we must position ourselves to receive His love.

In previous chapters we walked through the Outer Court and entered the Holy Place, where we first encountered the Golden Menorah. Now we come to the next piece of furniture in the Holy Place: the Table of Showbread, also called the bread of Presence or the bread of Face.

We read in Exodus 25:30, "You shall set the bread of the Presence on the table before Me at all times."

The table held twelve loaves, representing the twelve tribes of Israel. Every Sabbath the bread was replaced, and the priests would eat the old bread when the new loaves were set out. It was this sacred bread that David was permitted to eat when he was fleeing King Saul (1 Sam. 21:1–6). But what does this piece of furniture mean for us today? What is the prophetic significance of the Table of Showbread?

Note that this bread is not only called the bread of Presence; it is also called the bread of Face. That's because the bread was continually before the Lord's face.

> Every sabbath day he shall set it in order before the Lord continually; it is an everlasting covenant for the sons of Israel.
>
> —Leviticus 24:8

In the Holy Place, God gazed upon the twelve loaves, a prophetic picture of His people under His constant, loving watch. His face was always upon them. This reminds us that God is not a sometimes lover. He doesn't love us one day and ignore us the next. He loves us continually. He said, "I will never leave you nor forsake you" (Heb. 13:5, NKJV). When we're in a relationship with the Lord, His face is always upon us. As His beloved, we are the apple of His eye (Ps. 17:8; Zech. 2:8).

God wants to build our confidence in His love. The whole reason for the construction of the Tabernacle was because God wanted a relationship with Israel, and the Mishkan created a channel, or portal, through which His love could flow through Yeshua. This same God who encountered Israel at the Tabernacle is presently and continually reaching out to us today.

The world is filled with darkness. Pain and injustice are everywhere. Sometimes we may wonder, "If God is good, why does He allow so much suffering?" The devil wants to use what's happening in the world to keep us from recognizing that God is near. Father God is always here for us, but the enemy works hard to keep us from this truth. He wants to make us feel isolated and alone.

Have you ever noticed how often you're alone in your dreams? You wake up, thinking, "Wow, God wasn't with me in that dream. I didn't feel His presence." That's because

Satan is trying to make us feel like orphans. But the truth remains: God is with us even when we don't feel it. His presence always surrounds us.

Do you know that with every breath you breathe, you are taking in the love of God? Each breath you take is a gift from God. Each breath is God's kiss.

If we are to grow in our relationship with Father God, we need to understand down in our *kishkas*—deep down on the inside—that the Lord loves us. Even when someone else shows you love—a spouse, a friend, a child—that is God's love flowing through them because God is love. It is God's gift to you, further evidence of His abiding love.

Even though darkness is increasing in this world, God's love is still present. His eyes are always upon you, and He wants you to know "the breadth and length and height and depth" of His love, "that you may be filled up to all the fullness of God" (Eph. 3:18–19).

Feast on the Bread of Life

Yeshua declared, "I am the bread of life" (John 6:35). Just as the priests ate the physical bread of Presence in the Mishkan, we're called to spiritually eat Yeshua. This is what Communion, or the Lord's Supper, symbolizes.

> While they were eating, Jesus took some bread, and after a blessing, He broke it and gave it to the disciples, and said, "Take, eat; this is My body."
>
> —Matthew 26:26

We need to give our cravings and longings for satisfaction and fulfillment to Yeshua. We must feast on His presence, not on the flesh. When we feed on fleshly things, we weaken our ability to receive from the Spirit. If we don't guard our eyes—if we watch anything, listen to anything, let our minds wander wherever they want, and overindulge in food—we're going to be captivated and overcome by spirits of darkness and lose our awareness of Messiah's love.

But when we discipline our appetites by giving them to God, our weakness will be transformed into divine strength. We will ascend, overcome, and become truly happy. This phenomenon is highlighted by Messiah Jesus in John 6:51:

> I am the living bread that came down out of heaven; if anyone eats of this bread, he will live forever; and the bread also which I will give for the life of the world is My flesh.

It's Time to War

Now, on another but indirectly related note, consider this: Israel was given the Promised Land, but before they could possess it, they had to drive out the Amorites, Hittites, Jebusites, and other enemies. The land was theirs, but they still had to fight. It's the same for us today. God's love is real, but we must drive out the enemies that keep us from experiencing it.

The foes we must conquer are not necessarily physical. They are fear, passivity, lust, unbelief, selfishness, and the like. That's why seven times in Revelation 2 and 3, Yeshua said, "He that overcomes shall inherit these things." We must overcome the flesh. We must overcome undisciplined appetites. We must overcome the deceptions of the devil so that we can walk in the truth of God's love. The Table of Showbread prophetically reveals that God is with us, but we must war to believe and live in that truth.

Yeshua said, "I am with you always, even to the end of the age" (Matt. 28:20). We must fight the fight of faith to believe that as surely as the bread was before God's face in the Tabernacle, His eyes are always on us. He's always protecting us as we cling to Him.

Many times we look around and see all types of atrocities taking place in the world. But we need to take hold of the fact that even though a thousand may fall at our side and ten thousand at our right hand, no evil will befall us, for God is with us (Ps. 91:7, 10).

When the devil says, "God doesn't love you; He doesn't care," don't be passive. Confess God's Word and say, "God, You do love me, and I stand in that truth. By Your grace, I will not be defeated." When we affirm the truth and resist the enemy's lies, we overcome darkness and enter the light of God's presence.

You may be thinking, "But sometimes I don't *feel* God's love." If you can relate to that, I want to challenge you not to agree with the enemy. Feelings aren't facts, so don't say, "God, You don't love me," or "Lord, I don't think You've accepted me." Declare God's Word and say:

> Lord, I believe You love me (John 3:16).
>
> I believe You've forgiven my sins (Col. 2:13–14; 1 John 1:9).

I believe I'm accepted in the beloved (Eph. 1:6, KJV).

I believe You answer my prayers (1 John 5:14–15).

I believe You go with me wherever I go (Matt. 28:20).

I believe You've made me more than a conqueror in this life through Messiah Yeshua (Rom. 8:37).

Our emotions are like the clouds. They quickly come and go. While spending time high in the Rocky Mountains, I observed that the sun, clouds, and rain often alternated three times within one day. First, it was sunny for three hours. Then it got cloudy for a few hours. Next, the white clouds turned gray, pouring forth rain. And then it became sunny again, and the cycle continues. This is how our emotions are. Don't let Satan hold you captive to your emotions.

God's love is real and unchanging. We're in a fight. That's why Ephesians 6:12 tells us, "Our struggle is not against flesh and blood, but against the rulers, against the powers, against the world forces of this darkness, against the spiritual forces of wickedness in the heavenly places." But as we exercise faith in the truth, we'll come into a fuller experience of God's nearness.

Make Yeshua Lord

It's also critical to understand that to experience God's love deeply, we must live in surrendered obedience. We need to recognize when we're falling into sin—when we're being lazy, passive, or undisciplined. We must guard our mouths by speaking only that which gives life. We must be careful about the relationships we have and the way we treat people. We must be vigilant to take every thought captive to the obedience of Christ (2 Cor. 10:5). Our whole life must become about making Yeshua Lord.

When we choose to obey Him in every area and discipline ourselves to follow Him, He draws near to us, and we begin to experience God's love in a deeper way. This is the reward of obedience. It's why Yeshua said, "If anyone loves Me, he will keep My word; and My Father will love him, and *We will come to him and make Our abode with him*" (John 14:23).

James put it this way: "Draw near to God and He will draw near to you" (Jas. 4:8). As we separate ourselves from the ways of the world, we make room for God to dwell with us.

When we make Yeshua Lord, we experience the mystery of the bread of Presence. He discloses Himself to us, and we begin to see Him working, sense Him in our dreams, and watch Him go before us and move in our circumstances. He becomes real. That is the reward.

There is more to the Christian life than saying a sinner's prayer. Yeshua called us to make Him Lord. Salvation begins by having our sins forgiven, but if Jesus has really come into our lives, saying a prayer won't be enough. We'll have a hunger for God that compels us to love and obey Him.

So don't settle for hearing about God. Make it your aim to encounter Him daily. Yes, there will be times when you don't feel Him as powerfully. But if you continue seeking, continue warring, and continue drawing near, you will keep ascending, and He will become more real to you than ever before.

Chapter 7

PERPETUAL PRAYER: THE ALTAR OF INCENSE

As we continue moving further into the Tabernacle, the Mishkan, the last item of furniture we encounter in the Holy Place is the Altar of Incense, where the priest would perpetually burn incense unto the Lord.

> Moreover, you shall make an altar as a place for burning incense; you shall make it of acacia wood....Aaron shall burn fragrant incense on it; he shall burn it every morning when he trims the lamps. When Aaron trims the lamps at twilight, he shall burn incense. *There shall be perpetual incense before the Lord throughout your generations.*
>
> —Exodus 30:1, 7–8

As we have seen, everything in the Tabernacle has spiritual significance. Each item shows us how to progress into greater intimacy with the Lord, and the Altar of Incense is no exception. I believe it is a prophetic shadow of the prayer life of the believer, revealing Father God's desire that we commune with Him day and night. But before we go deeper, how do we know the Altar of Incense represents our prayers? David said in Psalm 141:2, "May my prayer be counted as incense before You; the lifting up of my hands as the evening offering."

The Book of Revelation gives us a glimpse of heaven where we see that the incense ascending before God's throne is mingled with the prayers of the saints.

> Another angel came and stood at the altar, holding a golden censer; and much incense was given to him, so that he might add it to the prayers of all the saints on the golden altar which was before the throne. And the smoke of the incense, with the prayers of the saints, went up before God out of the angel's hand.
>
> —Revelation 8:3–4

The Scriptures reveal that our prayers are like incense before the Lord. And the Altar of Incense in the ancient Tabernacle shows us that if we want to walk in victory and communion with God, prayer shouldn't be an occasional activity. It should be continual.

Exodus 30:8 says the incense before the Lord was to be *perpetual*. That is a strong word. It means ongoing and nonstop, which is why the apostle Paul said, "Pray without ceasing" (1 Thess. 5:17). The problem is that some of us think prayer only happens when we speak out loud. Yet prayer is much more than that. It is an internal awareness of God. It's living in communion with Him—thinking about Him, listening to Him, and reaching for Him with our spirit.

We see this in Yeshua's life. Right before He raised Lazarus from the dead, Messiah said, "Father, I thank You that You have heard Me. I knew that You always hear Me; but because of the people standing around I said it, so that they may believe that You sent Me" (John 11:41–42).

What we see here is that Yeshua prayed aloud for the sake of those around Him. But He was already communing with His Father on a deep, internal level because He lived in a perpetual state of prayer. To Him, prayer was walking in an awareness of His relationship with God. That's how simple prayer is.

Father God wants us to realize that He hears even the slightest whispers of our heart and understands the most minute motives and impulses of our hearts. It's good to pray out loud, but we must grab hold of the truth that God hears even the subtlest cries of our souls—and not only does He hear, but He responds.

As temples of the Holy Spirit (1 Cor. 3:16–17), we carry within us the incense that must rise continually before God. It should perpetually ascend from our spirits up to the Lord. For the believer, prayer is like oxygen. If we stop breathing, we die. Likewise, if we stop praying—talking to and with God—our spirits suffocate. An authentic prayer life isn't reflected by speaking to Him five or ten minutes each day; it's a life lived in constant communion.

Strange Incense

After giving Moses the instruction that the incense be burned continually, Yahweh issued a clear warning: "You shall not offer any strange incense on this altar" (Exod. 30:9). Then He gave Moses the precise recipe for the incense to be offered in the Tabernacle:

> Then the Lord said to Moses, "Take for yourself spices, stacte and onycha and galbanum, spices with pure frankincense; there shall be an equal part of each. With it you shall make incense, a perfume, the work of a perfumer, salted, pure, and holy."
>
> —Exodus 30:34–35

Only incense made with this exact blend of spices could burn on the altar. "Strange incense" would not be accepted. What this tells me is that not every kind of incense—or prayer—is acceptable to God. Certain prayers please God's heart and conform to His will, and others don't.

For example, Israel once begged God to give them a king so they could be like the other nations. This wasn't God's will for them because He wanted to be their king. But the people persisted, and eventually He gave them what they asked for. Sadly, many of Israel's kings led the people into idolatry. The nation ultimately split into two kingdoms, and the people were ruled by king after king who did evil in the sight of the Lord.

Beloved, be careful what you're praying for. God isn't pleased with prayers rooted in personal ambition or worldly desires. He's not interested in pampering the indulgences of our flesh. He's interested in conforming us to the image of Messiah Jesus. He's interested in giving us peace that surpasses all understanding (Phil. 4:7) and strengthening us in His love.

Father God is saying to us today: "Don't offer up strange incense. Don't pray for things that I don't desire for you. Don't pray to be famous in this world or to acquire wealth so you can achieve the American dream. Pray for Me to establish My kingdom in you. Pray that you'll know My love. Pray that you'll become steadfast in your walk with Me and live in victory."

I'm reminded of Solomon's prayer in 1 Kings 3, after the Lord appeared to him in a dream and said, "Ask what you wish Me to give you." Solomon prayed,

> Now, O Lord my God, You have made Your servant king in place of my father David, yet I am but a little child; I do not know how to go out or come in. Your servant is in the midst of Your people which You have chosen, a great people who are too many to be numbered or counted. So give Your servant an understanding heart to judge Your people to discern between good and evil. For who is able to judge this great people of Yours?
>
> —1 Kings 3:7-9

God was so pleased with Solomon's request that He gave him not only what he asked for—a wise and discerning heart—but both riches and honor too (vv. 12–13).

Prayers like Solomon's are not strange incense. They rise like a pleasing aroma before God's throne. Why? Because His Word has already revealed that they are His will.

The Prayers God Always Answers

Years ago, when I pastored a traditional church, we held a weekly prayer meeting. The same faithful people came every Wednesday night. And each time we asked for prayer requests, they would raise their hands and say the same things, like "Tim is driving down to Wisconsin, so let's pray for traveling mercies," or "Sally Ann is having gallbladder surgery," or "Sister So-and-So has a toothache, so she's going to the dentist."

God cares about all those issues (1 Pet. 5:7), and we should bring them before the Lord. But I believe God wants us to take our prayers deeper than those surface-level needs. Many times believers are going through the most horrendous circumstances in their lives: serious mental health challenges, a major relationship conflict, or some gross, immoral sin. Yet it seems that when Christians come together to pray, they address all the superficial concerns without ever getting into the deeper matters.

It's not that we shouldn't be praying about our visits to the dentist or for traveling mercies. Everything is important to bring to the Lord in prayer. But those aren't the innermost matters. The deepest things are inside: healing for our soul, wisdom, strength, revelation, love, holiness, and the like. When we begin to pray for these things, we will see results. Why? Because it's God's will for His presence, power, and purposes to be manifest in us. And when we pray according to His will, He always answers.

The apostle John wrote:

> This is the confidence which we have before Him, that, if we ask anything according to His will, He hears us. And if we know that He hears us in whatever we ask, we know that we have the requests which we have asked from Him.
>
> —1 John 5:14–15

You can pray for a new house, but you don't know for sure whether God will answer and give it to you. That's not something everyone can ask for and know it's been granted. But the prayers we *know* He will answer are the ones revealed as His will in His Word.

So let's look at some of these powerful prayers in Scripture, because we know if we pray these types of prayers, we'll be praying according to God's will and offering incense that is holy and acceptable to Him.

Praying for a Spirit of Wisdom and Revelation

One of the most powerful prayers in the Bible is found in Ephesians 1. The apostle Paul wrote,

> For this reason I too, having heard of the faith in the Lord Jesus which exists among you and your love for all the saints, do not cease giving thanks for you, while making mention of you in my prayers; that the God of our Lord Jesus Christ, the Father of glory, may give to you a spirit of wisdom and of revelation in the knowledge of Him.
>
> —Ephesians 1:15–17

Paul wasn't praying that the saints would have a bigger house or a nicer car. He was praying that we would receive something far more valuable: "a spirit of wisdom and of revelation in the knowledge of Him" (v. 17).

You might think more money is your answer, but that's not what is going to make you happy. The only people who think money is the answer are those who've never had it. I know that if you can't pay your bills or buy groceries, money would meet your immediate need. But money is not the answer to life's challenges. Knowing God is the answer. That's where peace, joy, and true identity come from. Solomon, the wisest human being to ever live, who experienced exceedingly abundant riches, wrote in Ecclesiastes 5:10, "He who loves money will not be satisfied with money, nor he who loves abundance with its income."

Paul continued in Ephesians 1:18:

> I pray that the eyes of your heart may be enlightened, so that you will know what is the hope of His calling, what are the riches of the glory of His inheritance in the saints.

Too often, all we see is the natural—what's happening on the surface. But when the eyes of our heart are enlightened, we begin to see through the lens of the Spirit. We start to understand who we are in Him. We stop being easily offended and living as victims because we know who we are: kings and priests in Messiah Jesus.

Yeshua was mocked, spit on, and beaten. Yet He looked at His persecutors and said, "Father, forgive them; for they do not know what they are doing" (Luke 23:34). He could forgive them because He knew who He was. His identity wasn't determined by how people treated Him. His eyes were enlightened, and He was secure in the Father's love.

When we pray with Paul from Ephesians 1, we're asking God to reveal who's inside us and what our destiny is: to realize that the Father chose us before the foundation of the world to be His. And that's a prayer He will always answer.

We see an interesting example of this principle in John 13, when Jesus washed the disciples' feet. The Scriptures say,

> Jesus, knowing that the Father had given all things into His hands, and that He had come forth from God and was going back to God, got up from supper, and laid aside His garments; and taking a towel, He girded Himself.
>
> —John 13:3–4

Jesus knew who He was. He knew He had come from God. He knew the Father loved Him and had given Him all things.

He knew His destiny. He didn't need anything from anybody, so He was free to concentrate on the needs of others. He could serve instead of needing to be served because He already was full. He already had everything He could ever want because He knew who He was. When we pray for the eyes of our understanding to be enlightened, we're asking God to anchor us in that same kind of confidence—to know who we are in Him, walk in our destiny as His sons and daughters, and see ourselves the way He does.

Paul continued, praying that Father God would enlighten you to know the reality of who you are in Him.

> And what is the surpassing greatness of His power toward us who believe. These are in accordance with the working of the strength of His might which He brought about in Christ, when He raised Him from the dead and seated Him at His right hand in the heavenly places.
>
> —Ephesians 1:19–20

Many Christians can't really fathom that the Spirit that raised Messiah Yeshua from the dead—that conquered death—lives in them. But if we ask to understand the power that's at work in our lives and how to walk in the fullness of the Ruach HaKodesh—the Spirit of God—that's a prayer we can be sure God will answer. So when we picture the incense and the smoke from the Altar of Incense inside the Tabernacle, let's picture these types of prayers.

Praying to Be Strengthened in Our Inner Man

There's another powerful prayer in Ephesians—this one in chapter 3. Paul writes,

> For this reason I bow my knees before the Father, from whom every family in heaven and on earth derives its name, that He would grant you, according to the riches of His glory, to be strengthened with power through His Spirit in the inner man, so that Christ may dwell in your hearts through faith; and that you, being rooted and grounded in love.
>
> —Ephesians 3:14–17

We live in a world where people are constantly working on their outward appearance. Everyone wants to be stronger, healthier, and more attractive. It's good and important to take care of your body. The Bible says that bodily discipline has value, but that spiritual discipline has even greater value because it is profitable both in this age and in the age to come (1 Tim. 4:8). So let's become more conscious of our inner dialogue with God than we are with our mortal, physical bodies.

God wants to empower us from the inside out. He wants us to ask Him to strengthen us with divine might in our inner man. Why? So that Messiah Jesus would dwell in our hearts—not as a concept but as a reality. So that we would be rooted and grounded not in religion or performance but in love.

A lot of people have big ideas about what they want to accomplish in life. But let me tell you, God is not concerned about us climbing the corporate ladder or achieving the American dream. He wants to see us strengthening our inner man so we will be able to lay hold of Him by faith—not just believe in Him as someone who is in heaven but understand that He's also in us and with us right now.

Paul goes on to pray that you "may be able to comprehend with all the saints"—not just with your intellect but to have real revelation—"what is the breadth and length and height and depth, and to know the love of Christ which surpasses knowledge, that you may be filled up to all the fullness of God" (Eph. 3:18–19).

This is what it's all about: to be filled up with the fullness of God. That's where real peace comes from. Pray this over your life each day. Talk to God. Ask Him to cleanse you of darkness and sin. Ask Him to heal you and make you whole. Ask Him to strengthen you by His Spirit with divine might so you'll be able to take hold of Him by faith, experience His reality, and comprehend the height, depth, and breadth of His love. I guarantee Father God will answer because His Word tells us this is absolutely His will for every child of God.

Praying to Be Filled with the Knowledge of His Will

Another prayer we should all be praying continually is found in the first chapter of the Book of Colossians.

> For this reason also, since the day we heard of it, we have not ceased to pray for you and to ask that you may be *filled with the knowledge of His will* in all spiritual wisdom and understanding.
>
> —Colossians 1:9

We're not going to walk in the knowledge of His will unless we're seeking it. This includes seeking to navigate all the relationships and circumstances of your life in a way that pleases Him. Walking in the knowledge of His will even includes the temporal and earthly affairs of your life. So if you need to know what job you should take, which congregation you should attend, or how to spend your money, ask the Lord.

When we pray to be filled with the knowledge of His will, we are asking to perceive the depths of Messiah Yeshua's heart in the Spirit. The Bible says no one knows the thoughts of God but the Spirit of God, and the Spirit has been given to us that we might freely know things of God (1 Cor. 2:11– 13). We need to know what God wants for our lives—how to make decisions, how to respond to people, how to manage our relationships and finances—and we can't figure that out with natural thinking alone. We need the Holy Spirit to reveal it to us.

Paul goes on to pray in Colossians 1:10 that you will have all spiritual wisdom and understanding "so that you will walk in a manner worthy of the Lord, to please Him in all respects, bearing fruit in every good work and increasing in the knowledge of God." As you know, some believers don't exercise wisdom in the way they handle themselves, talk, relate to people, manage their finances—and the list goes on. But Messiah Yeshua has become unto us wisdom from God, and righteousness, sanctification, and redemption (1 Cor. 1:30). And if we'll stop running ahead of God and instead wait on Him and say, "Holy Spirit, fill me with the wisdom and knowledge of God's will," we'll become like Daniel, to whom the king said, "Now I have heard about you that a spirit of the gods is in you, and that illumination, insight and extraordinary wisdom have been found in you" (Dan. 5:14).

Beloved, we want to "walk in a manner worthy of the Lord, to please Him in all respects, bearing fruit in every good work and increasing in the knowledge of God" (Col. 1:10). We want people to see that we have a spirit of excellency. We want to be like lights shining on a hill so that people will be attracted to Jesus because of the fruit they see in our lives.

Don't you want this kind of supernatural life? Don't you want the Holy Spirit to emanate from you? Don't you want whatever you touch to bear fruit? Well, the apostle Paul says when we're filled with the knowledge of God, we'll begin to bear fruit in every respect, and people will be blessed every time they encounter us. So when we picture the incense and smoke arising from the Altar of Incense in the Tabernacle, let it impress upon us to pray for what really matters—that we would continually grow in maturity and the knowledge of God.

Paul then prays that God will strengthen us "with all *power*, according to His glorious might, for the attaining of all *steadfastness* and patience; joyously giving thanks to the Father, who has qualified us to share in the inheritance of the saints in Light" (Col. 1:11–12). This means we won't be up one day and down the next. I know our emotions are constantly changing, but when we are strengthened by God's power, we'll be steadfast for every good work and walk in greater victory.

Talk to God about what you're thinking and how you're feeling. Share your innermost being with Him. God doesn't want you tossed around by every storm or circumstance. He wants you to be grounded and strong. He wants that for all His children. But we have to ask Him for it. We have to be in communion, sharing our lives with Him. Let's pray that He will strengthen us with divine might so we'll bear fruit in everything we do. Let's pray to have a spirit of steadfastness so we'll walk in a manner worthy of His call on us. These are prayers God has promised to answer.

Praying the Lord's Prayer

I could go on and on sharing scriptural prayers that God always answers. In fact, I explore these kinds of prayers at length in my book *The Key to Answered Prayer.* But in this chapter I want to share just one more prayer—one Messiah Himself taught us to pray: the Lord's Prayer.

Yeshua said,

> Pray, then, in this way: "Our Father who is in heaven, hallowed be Your name. Your kingdom come. Your will be done, on earth as it is in heaven. Give us this day our daily bread. And forgive us our debts, as we also have forgiven our debtors. And do not lead us into temptation, but deliver us from evil. [For Yours is the kingdom and the power and the glory forever. Amen."]
>
> —Matthew 6:9–13

This is one of the most well-known prayers in the world, but I believe many people repeat it without really understanding the depth of what Yeshua was teaching. So as we consider the fragrant and holy incense (representing our prayers) rising up to the Father in the Tabernacle, I want to look briefly at each line of this prayer to see what Messiah Jesus is revealing to us.

Yeshua begins by saying, "Our Father who is in heaven, hallowed be Your name." When we come before God, we must come with reverence. We're not talking to just anybody. We're addressing the Creator of the universe. He's holy, and He must be honored.

Years ago I heard a preacher on the radio invite listeners to try out "JC" (Jesus Christ). I understood that he was trying to connect with people, but to refer to Yeshua as JC is too familiar, and familiarity breeds contempt. The Scriptures say Yeshua couldn't do many miracles in His own town because they regarded Him just in the natural (Matt. 13:58). They were too familiar with Him.

The Lord says, "Those who honor Me I will honor" (1 Sam. 2:30). The Father needs to be revered. He's the Lord of glory. And when we come to Him, we need to approach Him with awe. In Scripture, when men encountered God—whether it was Moses at the burning bush, Isaiah in the Temple, or John on the island of Patmos—they fell on their faces in reverence. They had a revelation of God's holiness, and they responded in holy fear. That's what Yeshua is calling us to when He says, "Hallowed be Your name."

Then He says, "Your kingdom come. Your will be done, on earth as it is in heaven." This is a complete shift in how many of us pray. Too often our prayers are focused on our will—what we want God to do for us. But Yeshua is teaching us to first be concerned with *His will* being done in and through us, on earth as it is in heaven.

God's will is good. His will is that you would know

Him and experience His love. His will is that He be able to flow through you to build His kingdom. His will is that you be conformed to the image of His Son (Rom. 8:29) by denying yourself, taking up your cross, and following Him (Matt. 16:24–25). We ought to pray, then, to be conformed to the image of Messiah Jesus and to His will.

Messiah goes on to pray, "Give us this day our daily bread." This is where we bring the Lord our personal needs: physical, emotional, and spiritual. The Bible says, "In everything by prayer and supplication with thanksgiving let your requests be made known to God" (Phil. 4:6). This means that when we bring our requests to God, we must come with an attitude of gratitude, thanking Him first for all the things He's already done.

Oftentimes we come to the Lord with a list, asking for what we need now and want Him to do in the future. But we must first thank Him for the prayers He's already answered—the daily bread He's already provided—and then trust Him with today's needs. And after we bring Him both our material needs and the deeper issues of the heart, we can end by thanking Him in advance for what He's going to do.

Next Yeshua teaches us to pray, "And forgive us our debts, as we also have forgiven our debtors." This is one of the most serious parts of the prayer, because the forgiveness we receive is directly connected to the forgiveness we're willing to extend.

Yeshua told a parable in Matthew 18 about a servant who owed his master a great debt—one he could never repay. The master forgave him. But then that servant went out and demanded payment from someone who owed him a small amount. When the master found out, he was furious. He said, "Should you not also have had mercy on your fellow slave, in the same way that I had mercy on you?" (v. 33). Messiah Jesus said the man was handed over to the torturers. Why? Because he received forgiveness but refused to forgive.

You see, there are two laws in the universe: the law of the higher grace, or forgiveness, and the law of justice. If we want our sins to be forgiven, we must practice forgiving others. If we won't forgive others, if we want to hold an IOU over people's lives and demand justice from them, that's how the Lord is going to relate to us.

When He was on the cross, Yeshua looked at those who were persecuting Him and said, "Father, forgive them; for they do not know what they are doing" (Luke 23:34). The love of God flowed from Him so powerfully that the devil couldn't get in. If we want to have that kind of love flowing through our lives, we too must choose to forgive and release others.

That doesn't mean we minimize the wrong or pretend as if it didn't hurt. It doesn't mean we have to be best friends with the ones who wounded us. It means we don't set ourselves up as their judge and instead recognize that just as Jesus died for our sins, He died for theirs too. And if He died for their sins and forgave them, who are we to hold them in judgment?

Sometimes it's hard not to think about what someone did to us. Every time this happens, say, "*Father, I release them. I choose to forgive. I let go of bitterness and anger. Help me walk in Your love.*"

Then look immediately to the Lord and get drawn into thinking about Him. Picture Jesus on the cross, forgiving those who crucified Him.

You can't ignore this, beloved, because Yeshua said, "If you do not forgive others, then your Father will not forgive your transgressions" (Matt. 6:15). For the love and grace of God to flow through your life, you must choose mercy over judgment and release those who have sinned against you.

Then Yeshua says, "And do not lead us into temptation, but deliver us from evil." When I hear about people falling into sin and doing things we would consider atrocious, I always say before the Lord, "But for the grace of God, there go I." We don't know what temptations we're going to face tomorrow. Only God knows that. So we pray: "Lord, lead me not into temptation. Protect me. Keep me from stumbling. Deliver me from the enemy's traps. Help me walk in holiness today."

We pray this not just for today but even for tomorrow, because only the Father knows what we're going to face tomorrow. And if He doesn't keep us by His grace, we'll fall. We sometimes don't realize the battle we are in. When Yeshua said we should ask the Father to "deliver us from evil," He meant it. We need to be aware of how evil can work through our hearts and minds. When we have thoughts of hate, judgment, and condemnation toward others and ourselves, it's time to call out, "Father, deliver me from evil!"

Finally, the prayer ends with worship: "For Yours is the kingdom and the power and the glory forever. Amen." This is where we remember that all authority belongs to Him and He is worthy of our praise. The seraphim and divine beings around God's throne declare day and night, "Holy, holy, holy is the Lord God, the Almighty, who was and who is and who is to come" (Rev. 4:8; see also Isaiah 6:2–3). They never tire of praising Him because He is always doing something new.

A new revelation of His love, mercy, and goodness is forever unfolding. He's the same God, and He's constantly revealing His love to us in new ways. Whether He answers our prayers in the way we hoped, He is, was, and always will be worthy of our praise. We must be ever mindful of this reality.

A Life of Ceaseless Prayer

Through the Altar of Incense, the Lord is calling us to something greater than occasional prayers. He's inviting us into a lifestyle of communion with Him—a life of ceaseless prayer.

This isn't about saying the right words. It's about living with a heart that is continually reaching for Him. It's about becoming a dwelling place where holy incense never stops rising before His throne.

Don't waste your prayers asking God to satisfy your flesh. Don't offer strange incense on the altar. Instead, burn the sweet incense that's rooted in His Word and pray from an authentic heart wholly given over to Him. This kind of prayer life is powerful. It leads to intimacy with the Father and transforms us from the inside out.

As we draw near to God in this way and learn to pray according to His will, we shall see His promises fulfilled in our lives. Peace will replace anxiety. Confidence will silence fear. Power will overcome weakness. And the rivers of living water that Yeshua spoke of will begin to flow from our innermost being (John 7:38).

This is the mystery revealed through the Altar of Incense: Prayer is not something we do once in a while. It's a way of life that brings us into a deeper relationship with the Lord than we ever thought possible.

Chapter 8

OVERCOMING SPIRITUAL WARFARE: THE VEIL

As we go deeper into the Tabernacle, we move from the Holy Place—where we encountered the Golden Menorah, the Table of Showbread, and the Altar of Incense—toward the most sacred space of all: the Holy of Holies. This was where the presence of the Lord dwelled between the two cherubim on top of the Ark of the Covenant. But before the priest could enter that holy space—where he would hear God's voice and see His manifest presence—he first had to pass through a thick, heavy curtain called the Veil.

> You shall make a veil of blue and purple and scarlet material and fine twisted linen; it shall be made with cherubim, the work of a skillful workman....You shall hang up the veil under the clasps, and shall bring in the ark of the testimony there within the veil; and the veil shall serve for you as a partition between the holy place and the holy of holies.
>
> —Exodus 26:31, 33

The Holy of Holies was so sacred that only the high priest could enter it—and only once a year, on Yom Kippur, the Day of Atonement. Inside was the Ark of the Covenant, and within the Ark were the Ten Commandments—written not by Moses but by the very finger of God. The Lord gave the laws of the Torah, the first five books of the Bible, on Mount Sinai, and Moses wrote them down. But the Ten Commandments were different. God Himself inscribed them on tablets of stone. These commandments are so holy that they have formed the moral foundation of Western civilization. In fact, every major religion in the world draws from the moral law found in these ten truths written by God Himself.

Above the Ark were two golden statues of a class of celestial beings, or angels, called cherubim. The Hebrew word cherubim means "near ones." The cherubim are guardians of God's holy presence. They are first mentioned in the Bible in Genesis 3:24 after the Lord drove Adam and Eve out of the Garden of Eden for their rebellion—after they ate from the tree of the knowledge of good and evil.

> So He drove the man out; and at the east of the garden of Eden He stationed the cherubim and the flaming sword which turned every direction to guard the way to the tree of life.
>
> —Genesis 3:24

The visible presence of the Lord rested between the cherubim, and when the high priest entered the Holy of Holies to make atonement for the sins of Israel, the Lord would speak to him from between the golden cherubim.

To get into that sacred place, the priest had to pass through the thick, weighty Veil. Some say it was so heavy that it took several men to hang it. And here's something mysterious: There was no slit in the middle. So how did the high priest get through it?

According to some mystical Jewish traditions, the priest was supernaturally transported—or translated—through the Veil into the Holy of Holies. I don't know whether that, in fact, happened, but the Veil was clearly an obstacle since no one knows for certain how the priest got past it. This is why I believe that for us today, the Veil represents more than a physical barrier. It's a prophetic shadow of spiritual warfare. It points to the thick, heavy presence of the enemy we must press through if we are to enter the Holy of Holies, the place where we experience the deepest communion with God.

Today, many believers don't want to talk about spiritual warfare. They love the idea of God's blessings, but they don't want to deal with the devil. Some even think Satan and demons are only a problem for unbelievers. But that kind of thinking is like an ostrich sticking its head in the sand—and it's a dangerous deception.

The devil is real. Demons are real. And they absolutely target believers. If we're going to lay hold of God, we have to learn how to war in the spirit. We have to learn how to overcome. Seven times in Revelation, chapters 2 and 3, Yeshua says, "To him who overcomes." In Revelation 3:21, He declares, "He who overcomes, I will grant to him to sit down with Me on My throne, as I also overcame and sat down with My Father on His throne." We cannot walk in victory without learning how to defeat the enemy.

Building Strength Through Warfare

We even see this principle operating through the life of Yeshua. Before Jesus launched His public ministry, He was baptized in the Jordan River, and the moment was powerful. The heavens opened, the Holy Spirit descended on Him in bodily form like a dove, and He heard the Father say, "You are My beloved Son, in You I am well-pleased" (Luke 3:22).

But immediately after that, Yeshua was "led around by the Spirit in the wilderness for forty days, *being tempted by the devil*" (Luke 4:1–2).

Why would the Spirit of Elohim, the Spirit of God, orchestrate that? Why would He *lead* Yeshua into the wilderness to battle against Satan? It's because the Lord was preparing Him. God wanted to strengthen His Son through warfare so He would be able to exercise authority over darkness and be the Healer and Redeemer the Father had ordained Him to be.

After Jesus overcame the devil, Scripture says He returned from the wilderness "in the power of the Spirit" (Luke 4:14). He began to teach, and people marveled at His authority. But before that power was demonstrated publicly, Jesus first had to fight—and win—privately.

You see, even though He was the Son of God, Yeshua had to grow and learn. The Bible says He "kept increasing in wisdom and stature, and in favor with God and men" (Luke 2:52). He wasn't born into this world with a microchip in His head that downloaded everything He needed to know. God taught Him. And one of the ways the Father equipped Him for ministry was by having Him face the devil in spiritual warfare.

The Lord strengthened Yeshua in the Spirit as He learned how to overcome the enemy, and He's going to do the same for us. Father God strengthens our spiritual muscles by putting us in a position to war against the powers of darkness that seek to keep us from entering God's presence.

Beloved, we can go into the Holy Place in the spirit realm and encounter God. We can be led by His Spirit, represented by the Golden Menorah. We can know His presence is always with us, symbolized by the Table of Showbread. And we can commune with Him in constant prayer, as reflected at the Altar of Incense. But to get into the Holy of Holies—where we experience the closest, most intense fellowship with God—we must first overcome the evil one, just as Yeshua did. There is no other way. That's what the Bible says: "Our struggle is not against flesh and blood, but against the rulers, against the powers, against the world forces of this darkness, against the spiritual forces of wickedness in the heavenly places" (Eph. 6:12).

Recognize the Tactics of the Enemy

Our fight is not against a physical enemy. It's in the unseen realm. And the battleground where this war is often fought is in our thoughts.

Let me give you an example. In 1 Chronicles 21, the Bible says Satan moved David to take a census of Israel. David didn't know Satan was influencing him. He probably thought it was his own idea. Many scholars believe that David's decision to take a census was rooted in pride or a desire to trust in numbers and military power rather than the Lord. As a result of taking the census, David was disciplined by the Lord, and seventy thousand men of Israel died.

Now get this: David was deceived by a single thought, and that's still how the enemy works. He puts an idea in your mind, and if you don't recognize it and reject it, you'll potentially act on it. That's why we have to be vigilant.

For so many years, even as a Christian, I lived spiritually passive. I just accepted whatever thought entered my head. I didn't know I had the power to fight it. I would cry out to God for help and ask Him for mercy, but I didn't realize I had the power to reject the thought and focus on something else.

I want to encourage you to wake up! Ask the Holy Spirit to make you aware of what you're thinking about and reject the thoughts that are from your flesh or the enemy. As soon as you recognize a thought isn't from the Lord, come against it and say, "I reject you, Satan, in Jesus' name. Get out of my head!"

We see Jesus Himself doing this in Matthew 16:21–23:

> From that time Jesus began to show His disciples that He must go to Jerusalem, and suffer many things from the elders and chief priests and scribes, and be killed, and be raised up on the third day. Peter took Him aside and began to rebuke Him, saying, "God forbid it, Lord! This shall never happen to You." But He turned and said to Peter, "Get behind Me, Satan! You are a stumbling block to Me; for you are not setting your mind on God's interests, but man's."

There is something powerful in opening your mouth and talking back to the devil. When Yeshua was being tempted in the wilderness, every time Satan tried to bring Him into bondage, He countered Satan's strategy by speaking the Word of God (Matt. 4:3–11; Luke 4:3–13). In Jesus' day, people didn't carry around Bibles like we do now. Yeshua had the Scriptures memorized. You could say He had the Word hidden in His heart (Ps. 119:11). But when the devil came against Him, Yeshua didn't keep the Word in His heart. He didn't just think about Scripture—He spoke it. Every time

Satan came at Him, Jesus responded with "It is written" and quoted the Word of God (Matt. 4; Luke 4). And eventually the devil fled.

This is a principle throughout the Word of God. Romans 10:9 tells us that salvation happens when we *believe in our heart* and *confess with our mouth.* And Jesus said in Mark 11:23, "Truly I say to you, whoever says to this mountain, 'Be taken up and cast into the sea,' and does not doubt in his heart, but believes that what he says is going to happen, it will be granted him." We believe, and we speak. That's how we release the power of God.

If we don't get engaged in spiritual warfare and learn how to combat the lies of the enemy that enter our thoughts—if we don't allow ourselves to be trained by the Spirit of God to do spiritual warfare—we'll never penetrate the Veil and enter the Holy of Holies. Without penetrating through the powers of darkness into God's light, we will not be able to experience the fullness of the love, power, and beauty of God the way the Father wants us to.

Even as the Israelites had to drive out the Hittites, Amorites, Jebusites, Canaanites, and other enemies before they could enter the Promised Land, so you and I need to take authority over the powers of darkness if we're going to enter the abundant land of Messiah's Spirit. If we want to gain entrance into the Holy of Holies, we must learn to take authority over Satan, believe and confess God's Word, and pray that He strengthens us with divine might in our inner man so we can rise up and drive out the powers of evil, unbelief, and darkness.

The Tabernacle is a pattern for intimacy with God that

teaches us how we can know Him. And if we want to know Him in the fullest sense, we have to pierce the Veil! We can't stick our heads in the ground and pretend the devil is not real. Satan is real, and we need to understand how he's attacking us. We need to realize that the thoughts we think may not be coming from our subconscious mind or from other people. They may actually be from the enemy.

So we need to be alert. We need to discern when the devil is planting his lies in our minds and cast down every vain thought that exalts itself above the knowledge of God (2 Cor. 10:5). We need to overcome fleshly addictions, which a lot of times are being empowered by Satan. And we need to learn how to keep from being distracted from seeking the Lord, which, again, is often the enemy at work.

When we learn how to defeat the devil, we're going to encounter God's Spirit in a deeper way, even as the high priest passed through the Veil and experienced God's manifest presence in the Holy of Holies.

The Veil Has Been Torn

As previously discussed, under the old covenant, only the high priest could enter the Holy of Holies—and only once a year on the Day of Atonement, when he would pour the blood of the sacrifice on the altar for the forgiveness of the sins of the children of Israel. But when Yeshua died on the cross and said, "It is finished," everything changed.

> And Jesus cried out again with a loud voice, and yielded up His spirit. And behold, the veil of the temple was torn

> in two from top to bottom; and the earth shook and the rocks were split.
>
> —Matthew 27:50–51

God supernaturally ripped the Veil that isolated the Holy of Holies. And because that Veil has been torn, it's no longer just the high priest who can enter God's presence. Now, through the blood of Yeshua, everyone who has a relationship with Him has access by God's Spirit into His very presence—not once a year but anytime. Hallelujah!

Beloved, the high priest didn't casually stroll into the Holy of Holies. He had to get through the thick, heavy Veil—and so do we. Although the curtain may be torn, spiritual warfare remains real. We overcome not by our strength but by the blood of the Lamb, by the Word of our testimony, and by refusing to give the devil a foothold (Rev. 12:11; Eph. 4:27). The battle has already been won. God has given us the victory (1 Cor. 15:57). So let's press through—and enter in.

Chapter 9

ENCOUNTERING GOD'S PRESENCE: THE HOLY OF HOLIES

As we move beyond the Veil, we enter the Holy of Holies, the most sacred space on the planet. There God's visible presence dwelled above the Ark of the Covenant between the two cherubim. The high priest was permitted to enter this holy place only once a year, on Yom Kippur, to make atonement for the sins of the people. The priest would pour the blood of the sacrifice on the Mercy Seat atop the Ark of the Covenant, and the Lord would speak to him from between the cherubim.

We read about this most holy part of the Tabernacle in the Book of Exodus (Shemot in Hebrew):

> They shall construct an ark of acacia wood two and a half cubits long, and one and a half cubits wide, and one and a half cubits high.…You shall put into the ark the testimony which I shall give you. You shall make a mercy seat of pure gold, two and a half cubits long and one and a half cubits wide. You shall make two cherubim of gold, make them of hammered work at the two ends of the mercy seat.…You shall put the mercy seat on top of the ark, and in the ark you shall put the testimony which I will give to you. There I will meet with you; and from above the mercy seat, from between the two cherubim which are upon the ark of the testimony, I will speak to you about all that I will give you in commandment for the sons of Israel.
>
> —Exodus 25:10, 16–18, 21–22

According to the Book of Hebrews, inside the Ark of the Covenant were three sacred items: Aaron's rod that budded, a day's worth of manna, and the Ten Commandments (Heb. 9:4). There is some tension between what the Book of Hebrews says and what we read in the Torah. In Exodus 16:33–34 and Numbers 17:10, we read that the rod that budded and the jar of manna were near or in front of the Ark rather than inside it.

One possible reason for this discrepancy is that the Greek word used in Hebrews 9:4, *en he*, translated "in which," may not strictly mean "inside" but can also mean "with which" or "in association with." We know for certain that the Ten Commandments, written on tablets of stone, were inside the Ark. Whether Aaron's rod and the jar of manna were inside, in front of, or near the Ark, the fact that they were inside the Holy of Holies speaks to us of their importance. All three of these items carry prophetic significance for believers today.

Aaron's Rod That Budded

Aaron's rod was given as a sign of the Lord's authority after a group of Israelites rebelled against Moses's leadership. Korah, Dathan, and Abiram, along with 250 leaders of Israel, rose up against Moses and Aaron, saying, "You have gone far enough, for all the congregation are holy, every one of them, and the Lord is in their midst; so why do you exalt yourselves above the assembly of the Lord?" (Num. 16:3).

The Lord had chosen Moses to lead, and He selected Aaron to serve as high priest, but Korah and his followers despised that authority. This wasn't just a political uprising—it was a spiritual revolt against God's chosen leadership.

Moses fell on his face before the Lord, and God Himself judged the matter. The ground literally opened up beneath Korah, Dathan, and Abiram, swallowing them and their households alive. Fire from the Lord then consumed 250 others who had joined in Korah's mutiny. The rebellion was silenced, but the Lord wanted to give Israel a lasting symbol to remind them to respect His delegated authority.

So God told Moses to get a rod from each of the twelve tribes with the name of the tribe's leader on each one.

> It will come about that the rod of the man whom I choose will sprout.
>
> —Numbers 17:5

Aaron's name was written on the staff for the tribe of Levi, and the rods were placed before the Lord in the Tabernacle. The one whose rod God caused to supernaturally bud was the person He called to lead.

The next day, Aaron's rod had sprouted, blossomed, and produced ripe almonds while all the others remained the same (v. 8). This was God's undeniable sign that Aaron and the priesthood that would come through him were His chosen vessels.

The Lord then instructed Moses to place Aaron's rod before the Ark of the Covenant as a memorial to Israel:

> The Lord said to Moses, "Put back the rod of Aaron before the testimony to be kept as a sign against the rebels, that you may put an end to their grumblings against Me, so that they will not die."
>
> —Numbers 17:10

Aaron's rod became a reminder that God doesn't lead through democracy. The rebellious Israelites were grumbling against Moses because they wanted to lead. They wanted a vote. But whenever you have two visions, you have division. Multiple visions lead to chaos. That's why the armed forces have a strict line of authority. A soldier knows not to talk back to someone with a higher rank, especially in front of other troops. If such behavior was permitted, it would lead to chaos and an ineffective military. The troops know their responsibility is to carry out the instructions of their commanding officer.

The same is true in the kingdom of God. There must be respect for authority if God's kingdom is to be established on earth as it is in heaven.

Our God is a God of order. We see this in Numbers 2. The Lord gave Moses specific instructions for how the tribes should be *ordered* around the Tabernacle when they set up camp. And He dictated the order in which they were to depart when they broke camp.

Order holds the universe together, and it's no different in the body of Yeshua. I don't believe the church is supposed to be led democratically, with all the members voting on what color the carpet should be and what programs should be implemented. When God sets a leader in place, that leader becomes accountable to Him. Our responsibility is to pray for our leaders, ask God to give them wisdom and revelation, and believe that if correction is needed, the Lord will discipline or judge them.

Of course, we are not to obey leaders who tell us to do things that are immoral or illegal. Nor are we to revere human beings. But Romans 13:1 tells us there's no authority on earth that hasn't been established by God. So if we're going to be led by the Lord, we must understand that God has an established authority in the earth and that He works through the leaders He has set in place, and we must learn how to function under His ordained authority.

Consider the story of the centurion who came to Yeshua, asking Him to heal his servant. Jesus told the man He would go to his servant, but the centurion said, "Lord, I am not worthy for You to come under my roof, but just say the word, and my servant will be healed. For I also am a man under authority, with soldiers under me; and I say to this one, 'Go!' and he goes, and to another, 'Come!' and he comes, and to my slave, 'Do this!' and he does it" (Matt. 8:8–9).

When Jesus heard that, He marveled and said, "Truly I say to you, I have not found such great faith with anyone in Israel" (v. 10). The centurion recognized and understood Yeshua's authority.

Beloved, let's ask, pray, and believe God to work through His established authorities on the earth. It's when we lack faith in God that we think we have to be in control of every situation.

I know this is difficult, but the Scriptures tell us to respect not only leaders who are kind and believing, but even those who are unreasonable, for this pleases God (1 Pet. 2:18–20). Consider the apostle Paul in Acts 23 when he was brought before the Jewish Council. Paul initially was disrespectful to the high priest, but when he realized who Ananias was, Paul apologized and said, "I was not aware, brethren, that he was high priest; for it is written, 'You shall not speak evil of a ruler of your people'" (v. 5).

While we're often sensitive about avoiding sin, we sometimes forget that dishonoring God-ordained authority is no small matter in His eyes. Consider what happened with Noah. He got drunk, which was wrong. But two of his sons respected Noah's authority because he was their father and carefully walked backward to cover his nakedness without looking upon him. However, his other son, Ham, exposed his nakedness (Gen. 9:20–27).

Interestingly, the Bible doesn't tell us that the Lord rebuked Noah for being drunk, but He did rebuke the son who told his brothers of their father's nakedness. God judged that son for not respecting his father's authority.

The same thing happened when Aaron and Miriam complained about Moses because he married a Cushite woman. The Lord was upset with Aaron and Miriam for not respecting His authority on Moses, and He struck Miriam with leprosy.

In summary, Aaron's rod that budded is a prophetic reminder that if we are to enter the depth of God's holiness, we must learn to yield to and respect His ordained authority, not as unto men but as unto God.

The Jar of Manna

In addition to Aaron's rod, inside the Ark of the Covenant was a day's worth of manna.

> Then Moses said, "This is what the Lord has commanded, 'Let an omerful of it be kept throughout your generations, that they may see the bread that I fed you

> in the wilderness, when I brought you out of the land of Egypt.'" Moses said to Aaron, "Take a jar and put an omerful of manna in it, and place it before the LORD to be kept throughout your generations." As the LORD commanded Moses, so Aaron placed it before the Testimony, to be kept. The sons of Israel…ate the manna until they came to the border of the land of Canaan.
>
> —EXODUS 16:32–35

By having the Israelites save a jar full of this supernatural bread they called manna, the Lord was giving them a continual reminder of His supernatural provision. For forty years in the wilderness, God fed them each day with bread from heaven. Every morning like clockwork, except on the Sabbath, the manna supernaturally appeared on the ground. They were instructed to gather only enough manna for one day, except on the sixth day. If they tried to gather more than one day's worth of manna, it would go foul and become infested with worms. But on the Sabbath, God supernaturally preserved the extra manna that He instructed them to gather on the sixth day so that the Israelites could rest on the seventh day. (See Exodus 16:16–24.)

For believers today, the manna in the Ark is a prophetic reminder that if we are to go all the way with God and fulfill His purpose, we have to trust Him to do the supernatural in our lives. Why do I say this? Because Israel only entered the Promised Land through God's supernatural provision. The manna was supernatural. The fact that it did not become foul but was preserved on Shabbat (the Sabbath) was supernatural.

To lay hold of and enter into what God has prepared for us, we must step out in faith and trust Him to do the supernatural in our lives. If we feel like we need to map out each step before we obey, making sure we're dotting the i's and crossing the t's, we will never enter His fullness.

It took a lot of faith for Peter to walk on the water. It took faith for those disciples to cast their nets again after fishing all night and catching nothing. It always takes faith to depend on God's supernatural provision—to believe that if we do what He says, He will meet us and supply our needs. If we think, "I'm not going unless it all makes sense first," we're never going to arrive in His promised land. But when we believe we have a supernatural God who's able to supply all our needs according to His riches in glory in Messiah Jesus (Phil. 4:19), we'll find the courage to step out and go all the way with Him.

I experienced this personally back in 1978, when the Lord supernaturally revealed Himself to me in a dream. I had to leave what my Jewish culture had told me was true—that you can't be a Jew and believe in Jesus. To my community, it was a shameful thing to follow Yeshua. But I had to step out of what was familiar and trust that as I obeyed, God would supernaturally bless me.

Yeshua promised, "Truly I say to you, there is no one who has left house or brothers or sisters or mother or father or children or farms, for My sake and for the gospel's sake, but that he will receive a hundred times as much now in the present age, houses and brothers and sisters and mothers and children and farms, along with persecutions; and in the age to come, eternal life" (Mark 10:29–30).

I had to believe those words. I had to trust that by stepping out and following the Lord—even though it meant losing my family—God was going to abundantly bless and reward me. And He has. Today, I honor and bless the earthly family I came from, but I recognize that following Yeshua came at a cost. I had to trust Him step by step. And you are called to do the same—to believe that as you follow Him, He will abundantly bless you by His Spirit and through His Son.

You may remember that once the children of Israel entered the Promised Land, the manna ceased. Why? Because they no longer needed it. They had entered the Promised Land of milk and honey, and God's blessing now came to them through more natural means. But the jar of manna serves as a sign that if we're ever in a place where we're following God and there is no natural means by which our need can be met, Father God will supply it supernaturally. He has done this for me many times, and He will do it for you.

The Ten Commandments

Finally, inside the Ark of the Covenant was the most sacred object of all: the two stone tablets containing the Ten Commandments, written by the very finger of God (Exod. 31:18). The Lord commanded Moses:

> You shall put into the ark the testimony [the Ten Commandments] which I shall give you.
>
> —Exodus 25:16

When Yahweh gave the Ten Commandments—called in Hebrew the Ten Words—to the Israelites who were gathered at the base of Mount Sinai, they were terrified by His power and glory.

> So it came about on the third day, when it was morning, that there were thunder and lightning flashes and a thick cloud upon the mountain and a very loud trumpet sound, so that all the people who were in the camp trembled.... Now Mount Sinai was all in smoke because the Lord descended upon it in fire; and its smoke ascended like the smoke of a furnace, and the whole mountain quaked violently.
>
> —Exodus 19:16, 18

When the Lord spoke aloud at Mount Sinai, Jewish tradition tells us that the Lord spoke the Ten Commandments in seventy different languages at the same time. This idea corresponds to the seventy nations of the earth recorded in Genesis 10. In other words, God gave the Ten Words, or Ten Commandments, which He engraved on the stone tablets to the whole world. Those tablets were ultimately placed inside the Ark of the Covenant as a perpetual reminder of who God is and His covenant with Israel.

Through the centuries, the Ten Commandments have become the bedrock of Western civilization's moral code. The Lord delivered the world out of barbarianism by these ten ethical laws. The commandments have shaped legal systems and set universal principles of justice and compassion, and they remain as relevant today as when they were given.

In giving the Ten Commandments, God wasn't just dictating a list of dos and don'ts. He was revealing His nature and character. When we view God's commandments spiritually, we see that they still apply to our lives. For example, when the Lord said, "I am the God who brought you out of the land of Egypt," He was saying, "This is why you should obey Me—because I'm the God who loves you so much that I brought you out of bondage." And when He instructed His people to have no other gods before Him (Exod. 20:3), He was showing us the way to walk in victory, which is by giving Him our exclusive devotion. He knew that anything we trust in or desire above Him—success, relationships, acceptance, human wisdom, and so on—would never truly satisfy and ultimately lead to bondage. So He revealed a more excellent way through His commandments.

Each of the Ten Commandments has a current prophetic application for us today. Scan this QR code or visit RabbiSchneiderBooks.com/tabernacle/resources to take a deeper dive into how each one applies to our lives.

The Ten Commandments, which were placed inside the Ark, represent the *covenant relationship* God desires to have with His people.

God's Presence Between the Cherubim

On top of the Ark of the Covenant was the Mercy Seat, where the blood of the sacrifice was poured out once a year on Yom Kippur (the Day of Atonement) to atone for the sins of Israel. When the high priest went into the Holy of Holies on Yom Kippur, God would speak to him out of His manifest presence, which dwelled above the Mercy Seat between the two cherubim.

> You shall put the mercy seat on top of the ark, and in the ark you shall put the testimony which I will give to you. There I will meet with you; and from above the mercy seat, from between the two cherubim which are upon the ark of the testimony, I will speak to you.
>
> —Exodus 25:21–22

Beloved, this is where our journey through the Tabernacle leads—to the place where we experience the very presence and voice of God. Unlike the ancient high priest who encountered God's presence only once a year, you and I as believers in Yeshua have His Spirit dwelling within us daily. His presence is no longer hidden behind a veil; it is our constant companion.

The same Spirit who hovered above the Mercy Seat now lives inside us, and we can hear Him speaking to us and be led by Him day by day. Remember, Yeshua said, "My sheep hear My voice" (John 10:27). That doesn't mean we're going to hear the audible voice of God every day. His "voice" is often a gentle nudge or an inner witness. But as we make Messiah Jesus the absolute center of our lives, He is going to teach us by His Spirit how to discern His voice and make us sensitive to the feeling of His Spirit in our spirit, or our inner man.

I call this intuitive listening. As we pay attention to the inner witness of the Holy Spirit—noticing whether we have peace about going in a particular direction or sense a check that something isn't right—over time we'll find ourselves being led successfully by the supernatural presence of God.

The Spirit of God is within us, and He speaks to us from within, either giving us a check in our spirit or a release of peace. Yet if we're not in touch with Him inside, we'll just push right ahead, do our own thing, and get ourselves into trouble. But as we learn to wait on God, be still before Him, and yield to His Spirit, we'll become better able to hear His voice and perceive His will.

Even as the children of Israel were led in the wilderness by the pillar of fire by night and the divine glory cloud by day, you and I must learn to be led by God's Spirit. We read in Numbers 9–11 that whenever the fire and the glory cloud rested over the Tabernacle, the Israelites camped in that spot. But when they lifted, the people would move as well. Sometimes they stayed in one place for two days, sometimes for two months, or sometimes even for two years. But no matter how long they had been camped in one location, whenever the fire and the cloud moved—whether in the morning, in the afternoon, or at night—the people of Israel broke camp and followed it.

So it must be for us today. The fire and the cloud of the Holy Spirit have come into our lives, and if we are going to enter His fullness, we must be led by God's Spirit. "For all who are being led by the Spirit of God, these are sons of God" (Rom. 8:14).

The Veil has been torn. The Spirit has been poured out. God is not far off—He is here, within you. And the more you yield to Him, the more His voice will become clear, His presence tangible, and His power alive in your life.

Part II

WORSHIP IN THE TABERNACLE

Chapter 10

SACRIFICIAL WORSHIP

At this point in our journey through the Tabernacle, I want to pause and reflect on where the Lord has brought us thus far. We entered through the Gate—the one way in—and explored the Bronze Altar and Brass Laver, where our sins are forgiven and we are cleansed. We then moved into the Holy Place, where we encountered the Golden Menorah, representing God's Spirit; the Table of Showbread, which reminds us of God's love and abiding presence; and the Altar of Incense, representing the sweet aroma of our prayers. Finally, we went through the Veil, a symbol of the spiritual warfare we must press through to experience a deeper fellowship with God. Once through the Veil, we entered the Holy of Holies, where the manifest presence of God dwelled above the Ark of the Covenant.

The Tabernacle, as we have seen, is a blueprint for developing intimacy with God. But it does more than show us how to enter His presence. It also reveals a pattern for authentic worship.

The Hebrew word for worship is *shachah,* and it's actually an action word because worship is something we do. It's active and alive. In the Tabernacle—the Mishkan—the ancient Israelites worshipped the Lord primarily through the offering of sacrifices. The worship through sacrificial offerings not only pointed to Messiah Jesus but were also a foreshadowing of how you and I are to walk with God.

In today's self-centered culture, many believers focus only on their own needs and desires when they approach God.

We often attend church in a posture to receive, seeking to be blessed by the music or the sermon. But when we study the Tabernacle, we discover a strikingly different way of worship. The Israelites approached the Lord with reverence and humility. One of the meanings of the word *worship* is to prostrate oneself, and that's what the Israelites did. They didn't come to the Tabernacle primarily to receive or to be blessed. They came with an offering to worship and bless Yahweh. The Lord was at the center, not their own needs.

Why Sacrifice?

The five main sacrifices offered in the Tabernacle are outlined in the Torah (the first five books of the Old Testament). God required them of His people. After giving the blueprint for the Tabernacle, He said in essence, "I want you to draw near to Me because I desire to dwell with you, and when you draw near, I want you to offer Me these sacrifices."

Why did the Lord call His people to come before Him with sacrifices? Is God an egomaniac who constantly needs to be told how great He is? Is He insecure, leading Him to require regular pats on the back? God forbid!

Here is what is really going on. The Hebrew word often translated *offering* or *sacrifice* is *korban*, and it means "to draw close" or "to draw near." Through the Tabernacle God showed the Israelites that the way to be close to Him was to come to Him with a sacrifice. He didn't require these offerings just to have the Israelites give something up. Rather, they were His invitation to intimacy. In posturing themselves correctly before their Maker, they opened up the channel through which they were to receive.

Still today, our God is inviting His people to draw near through sacrificial worship. He is calling us to lay down our lives and make Him the center of all things. The Lord doesn't command us to worship Him just because He wants us to praise Him. Deep in His heart, He has a reflexive desire to bless us, and it's only when we make Him the center of our lives that He can do so.

Romans 12:1–2 tells us we are to present our very lives to Him as "a living and holy sacrifice, acceptable to God, which is [our] spiritual service of worship." Worship is the giving up of ourselves, the abandoning of our desires, to make Him the focus of our lives. When we surrender to Him in this way, we step closer to His presence and position ourselves to experience Him, dwell with Him, and, as a result, be blessed by Him.

The Priesthood of Believers

Although the ancient Israelite worshippers brought the sacrifices to the Tabernacle, it was the priest who offered them to God. Throughout history those who functioned as priests has changed. At one time the firstborn in every Israelite household was seen as a priest of the Lord. Then that role was transferred to the Levitical priesthood, who were the descendants of Aaron (Num. 3:11–13).

But today the priesthood operates in the life of every child of God who has been redeemed by the blood of Yeshua. Revelation 20:6 declares, "Blessed and holy is the one who has a part in the first resurrection; over these the second death has no power, but they will be priests of God and of Christ and will reign with Him for a thousand years." You are a priest. Jesus purchased you by His own blood to be unto Him a kingdom of priests (Rev. 1:6, 5:10). Hallelujah!

And what is a priest? In the Hebrew Bible (the Old Testament), the priest had three key responsibilities: to draw near to God, to offer sacrifices to Him, and to bless others. Spiritually, we are called to do the same today.

1. To draw near

First, as priests of God we've been granted the right and privilege to draw near to Yahweh. Jesus said, "No one can come to Me unless the Father who sent Me draws him" (John 6:44). As chosen children of God who have been given the inheritance of the priest, we have been called to draw near to Him and go boldly before the throne of grace (Heb. 4:16).

2. To offer sacrifices

Second, as priests we are called to offer sacrifices. When we study those throughout Scripture whom God called to Himself, we see that as He brought them near, He called upon them to offer a sacrifice. He called on Abraham to sacrifice his promised son, Isaac (Gen. 22). He told Jacob to move from Shechem to Bethel and build an altar there, representing his return to a life of wholehearted devotion to God (Gen. 35:1–4). After Solomon became king, one of the first things he did was present a thousand burnt offerings to God at Gibeon (1 Kings 3).

Again and again in Scripture, people presented sacrifices

to God as a way to draw near and express their devotion to Him, and our sacrifices today continue to open the door for intimacy with Him. But we must realize that offering sacrifices to God is not just a matter of raising our hands in a church service. A sacrifice costs us something. When we give something up to honor the Lord because of our love for Him, He responds to that and draws near to us.

God is worthy of nothing less than our best. When we surrender something to God, we're not losing anything. Yes, we're giving something up, but we're gaining something so much greater from the realm of the eternal.

Remember what the apostle Paul said about his life:

> If anyone else thinks he may have confidence in the flesh, I more so: circumcised the eighth day, of the stock of Israel, of the tribe of Benjamin, a Hebrew of the Hebrews; concerning the law, a Pharisee; concerning zeal, persecuting the church; concerning the righteousness which is in the law, blameless.
>
> But what things were gain to me, these I have counted loss for Christ. Yet indeed I also count all things loss for the excellence of the knowledge of Christ Jesus my Lord, for whom I have suffered the loss of all things, and count them as rubbish, that I may gain Christ…that I may know Him and the power of His resurrection, and the fellowship of His sufferings, being conformed to His death, if, by any means, I may attain to the resurrection from the dead.
>
> —PHILIPPIANS 3:4–8, 10–11, NKJV

Paul gave up everything he had—his former life, his credentials, his ethnic pride as an Israelite. He gave it all up as a sacrifice to the Lord, and he said he counted it all as rubbish that he might gain Messiah Jesus.

In much the same way, when you and I offer our lives as sacrifices to the Lord, we gain everything. It's like the woman in John 12 who poured out perfume worth a year's wages onto Yeshua's feet. She may have appeared to lose something in the natural, but she gained Jesus.

3. To bless others

The third role of the priest is to bless others. We see this illustrated in Leviticus 9.

> Now it came about on the eighth day that Moses called Aaron and his sons and the elders of Israel; and he said to Aaron, "Take for yourself a calf, a bull, for a sin offering and a ram for a burnt offering, both without defect, and offer them before the Lord."...He also presented the burnt offering, and offered it according to the ordinance. Next he presented the grain offering, and filled his hand with some of it and offered it up in smoke on the altar, besides the burnt offering of the morning....*Then Aaron lifted up his hands toward the people and blessed them.*
>
> —Leviticus 9:1–2, 16–17, 22

After Aaron presented the sacrifices to the Lord, he lifted up his hands and blessed the people. So too as believers and priests of Yahweh today, our role is to allow ourselves to be used by Him to bless others. He's called you to be "a chosen race, a royal priesthood, a holy nation, a people for God's own possession, so that you may proclaim the excellencies of Him who has called you out of darkness into His marvelous light" (1 Pet. 2:9). Beloved, you and I carry an anointing to bless others. We carry God's Spirit, and as we abide in Him and walk in the truth, we are literally empowered to impart a dynamic blessing to those around us.

God's Response to Sacrifice

In the Tabernacle, consider what happened when Aaron, the high priest, presented an offering that was pleasing to the Lord. The glory of God fell. Heaven touched earth. Looking again at Leviticus 9, we read:

> Then Aaron lifted up his hands toward the people and blessed them, and he stepped down after making the sin offering and the burnt offering and the peace offerings. Moses and Aaron went into the tent of meeting. When they came out and blessed the people, *the glory of the Lord appeared to all the people. Then fire came out from before the Lord and consumed the burnt offering and the portions of fat on the altar*; and when all the people saw it, they shouted and fell on their faces.
>
> —Leviticus 9:22–24

Do you see the pattern? The Tabernacle was built as a place for Yahweh to dwell among His people. Inside the Tabernacle, the priest offered the sacrifices, and God responded by drawing near. The glory of the Lord appeared to all the people.

Then fire came out of heaven and consumed the sacrifices. That means the Lord accepted the offerings and received them as a love gift. He manifested Himself to them because He was so pleased that they humbled themselves before Him, offering sacrifices not for what they could get from Him, but simply because He was worthy of their love and reverence. So too when we make Yahweh the center of our lives and give Him our wholehearted devotion, He responds by drawing near to us and manifesting His presence.

Let's consider another example. In Exodus 40, Moses put everything in place in the Tabernacle exactly as the Lord commanded him. Then "He set the altar of burnt offering before the doorway of the tabernacle of the tent of meeting, and offered on it the burnt offering and the meal offering, just as the Lord had commanded Moses" (Exod. 40:29).

Notice what happened as a result:

> Then the cloud covered the tent of meeting, and the glory of the Lord filled the tabernacle. Moses was not able to enter the tent of meeting because the cloud had settled on it, and the glory of the Lord filled the tabernacle.
>
> —Exodus 40:34–35

Beloved, if you want the Lord to reveal Himself to you and fill you with His Spirit, offer Him your life as a sacrifice. Reject teachings that make you the center of the story. God does not exist just to make us rich in this world and help us achieve all our dreams. Yes, the Lord blesses His people, but walking with God isn't about attaining earthly success. It's about making Him the center of our lives. Yeshua said, "He who has lost his life for My sake will find it" (Matt. 10:39).

We must offer the Lord a sacrifice that costs us something. King David understood this. In 2 Samuel 24, David wanted to build an altar and offer sacrifices to the Lord on a threshing floor that belonged to Araunah the Jebusite. So David went to Araunah and asked to buy the threshing floor, an area used to separate grain, but Araunah told him he could have it and even offered to give him oxen and wood.

But David said, "No, but I will surely buy it from you for a price, for I will not offer burnt offerings to the Lord my God which cost me nothing" (v. 24). David said in essence, "I'm going to show God how precious He is to me by paying a costly price for whatever I give to Him."

Look what God did as a result:

> So David bought the threshing floor and the oxen for fifty shekels of silver. David built there an altar to the LORD and offered burnt offerings and peace offerings. *Thus the Lord was moved by prayer for the land, and the plague was held back from Israel.*
>
> —2 SAMUEL 24:24–25

The Lord responded to David's sacrifice by stopping the plague that was about to come upon Israel. If you want to be blessed by the Lord and protected from the plagues that threaten your life, present yourself as "a living and holy sacrifice, acceptable to God, which is your spiritual service of worship" (Rom. 12:1).

Whether we realize it or not, we all worship something. Those who claim not to believe in God have given their lives over to something. We either offer ourselves as a sacrifice to God or as a sacrifice to sin—"for all that is in the world, the lust of the flesh and the lust of the eyes and the boastful pride of life, is not from the Father, but is from the world (1 John 2:16).

Think about those addicted to alcohol. They're offering their bodies as a sacrifice to alcohol, getting drunk, damaging their health, and risking their future. The same is true of those addicted to drugs, lust, pornography, social media—and the list goes on. In one way or another, we all surrender to something.

When we put our heavenly Father at the center of everything, surrendering ourselves wholly to Him, holding nothing back, His fire consumes us—purifying, refining, and filling us with His Spirit.

Five Types of Sacrifices

Scripture records five major sacrifices that Yahweh commanded the Israelites to offer in the Tabernacle:

1. The burnt offering (Lev. 1)
2. The grain (or meat/meal) offering (Lev. 2)
3. The peace offering (Lev. 3)
4. The sin offering (Lev. 4)
5. The trespass (or guilt) offering (Lev. 5–6)

These offerings were presented in a specific order. First were the burnt, grain, and peace offerings. When these offerings were burned on the altar, the smoke that ascended was a *sweet-smelling* savor to Yahweh. In contrast, the sin and trespass offerings were not referred to as a pleasing aroma to

God. Why? Because sin is ugly and offensive to God—it separates us from Him.

These five offerings are prophetic shadows—double shadows, in fact. They not only point us to Messiah Jesus but also reveal how we should come before God.

First, these offerings are a shadow of Yeshua, who fulfilled each one through His perfect life and ultimate sacrifice on the cross. His life reflects the divine order of these sacrifices: the "sweet-smelling" offerings that symbolize His perfect obedience and holiness, and then the guilt offerings, representing His atoning work on the cross.

Ephesians 5:2 affirms that Yeshua "gave Himself up for us, an offering and a sacrifice to God as a fragrant aroma." Jesus, the beautiful, blameless Lamb of God, came into the earth and lived a perfect life before God. His life—marked by complete obedience—was a pleasing aroma unto the Lord. Then at the end of His earthly ministry, this perfect One who lived a perfect life offered Himself up as a sin and trespass offering for humanity, bearing the penalty of our sins.

By giving Himself up to the Father for us on the cross, He became the culmination of all these sacrifices. This is why Yeshua declared the following: "Do not think that I came to abolish the Law or the Prophets; I did not come to abolish but to fulfill. For truly I say to you, until heaven and earth pass away, not the smallest letter or stroke shall pass from the Law until all is accomplished" (Matt. 5:17–18).

Hebrews 10:1 emphasizes that the Law "since it has only a shadow of the good things to come and not the very form of things, can never, by the same sacrifices which they offer continually year by year, make perfect those who draw near." But Yeshua by offering up His own life has "perfected for all time those who are sanctified" (Heb. 10:14).

Second, these sacrifices are a shadow of our worship. The Israelites actually presented the offerings to the Lord in the opposite order they're revealed in Scripture. We read in Leviticus 9 that the Israelites didn't begin with the burnt, grain, and peace offerings; they first presented their sin offering. Only after addressing their sin could they proceed to the offerings that were a fragrant aroma unto Yahweh. This order teaches us a timeless truth: We must first confront our sin before we can experience true worship and intimacy with God.

It's also important to understand that an Israelite identified with his sacrifice. For example, the worshipper laid his hand on his burnt offering "that it may be accepted for him to make atonement on his behalf" (Lev. 1:4). The offering became an extension of his heart so that as the sin offering was presented to the Lord, it was as if the Israelite's own sin was taken away and his life was being fully consecrated to Yahweh.

Authentic worship mirrors this kind of reverent awe and total devotion. There was just one way to enter the Tabernacle, and there is only one way to worship God: His way, not our own way. True spirituality begins with recognizing who God is and relating to Him properly—not as someone who exists just to give us everything we want but as the One who deserves to be worshipped because of how beautiful, awesome, incredible, and good He is.

In the next several chapters, we will look at each of these

five primary offerings and what they reveal about how we are to come before God in worship today—not as someone we can use to satisfy our own lusts, but as the Holy One who should be loved and revered with a holy fear simply because of who He is.

Chapter 11

A SACRIFICE OF SURRENDER: THE BURNT OFFERING

THE FIRST OFFERING revealed in the Book of Leviticus is the burnt offering:

> Then the LORD called to Moses and spoke to him from the tent of meeting, saying, "Speak to the sons of Israel and say to them, 'When any man of you brings an offering to the LORD, you shall bring your offering of animals from the herd or the flock. If his offering is a burnt offering from the herd, he shall offer it, a male without defect; he shall offer it at the doorway of the tent of meeting, that he may be accepted before the LORD.'"
>
> —LEVITICUS 1:1–3

The Hebrew word for "burnt offering" is *olah*, which means to ascend or go up. What set this offering apart was that the entire animal—the head, the skin, the inner organs, all of it—was burned up on the altar, its aroma rising to Yahweh as a sweet-smelling savor:

> And the priest shall offer up in smoke *all of it* on the altar for a burnt offering, an offering by fire of a soothing aroma to the LORD.
>
> —LEVITICUS 1:9

God required all the offering, not just part of it. And this is exactly what He desires from us today: our full surrender and total devotion. If we want to draw close to Him, we can't hold anything back. He wants our everything.

This is the kind of commitment Abraham demonstrated. In the Book of Genesis (Bereshit in Hebrew), God said to Abraham:

> Take now your son, your only son, whom you love, Isaac, and go to the land of Moriah, and offer him there as a burnt offering on one of the mountains of which I will tell you.
>
> —Genesis 22:2

Isaac was the only son of Abraham's wife, Sarah, and the fulfillment of a long-awaited promise (Heb. 11:17–19). Yet Abraham was willing to place Isaac on the altar, an act that symbolized Abraham's utter abandonment to Yahweh.

Beloved, the Lord is not moved by our saying, "I'll follow You, but I want to keep this part of my life under my control." That's what Ananias and Sapphira did in Acts 5. They claimed to have given God everything, but in truth they reserved a part for themselves, and they were judged for it.

Help us all, Lord! We want to love You completely. Forgive us and sanctify us. Deliver us, Father, for not trusting You and loving You with our whole being.

Entire Consecration

The commandments (*mitzvot*) in the Torah addressed every aspect of the Israelites' lives—what they ate, how they dressed, instructions on harvesting—everything. They were God's way of showing them that He required their complete consecration.

The Lord hasn't changed. He still desires every aspect of our lives—even down to the way we present ourselves.

For believers in Yeshua, it is inappropriate for us to dress in a way that draws people to our flesh. The apostle Paul wrote, "If you arc living according to the flesh, you must die; but if by the Spirit you are putting to death the deeds of the body, you will live" (Rom. 8:13). I'm not saying we can't dress attractively. But there is a way to clothe ourselves that brings glory to God.

When the Temple was built, the high priest wore garments that the Scriptures say were "for glory and for beauty" (Exod. 28:2, 40). But he didn't dress in a way that drew attention to his body parts. He was clothed in a manner that honored God.

Animals live by their natural instincts, but God wants mankind to reign over our base impulses. He doesn't want us relying on the power of our flesh—our sensuality, intellect, or personality—to manipulate people so we can get by in this world. He calls us to yield every part of ourselves to Him.

In the Torah, God instructed the children of Israel to wear the *tzitzit*—the fringes on the four corners of a Jewish prayer shawl—as a continual reminder of their covenant with Him (Num. 15:38–41). These fringes are what the woman with the hemorrhage for twelve years reached for when she touched the hem of Yeshua's garment (Mark 5:25–34). In a sense, the *tzitzit* functioned like the WWJD ("What Would Jesus Do?") bracelets popular in the 1990s. They were a visible reminder, seen throughout the day, that the wearer belonged to the Lord and was called to walk in His ways, not straying to the left or right but letting His truth reign in their lives.

My point is that just as the burnt offering, the *olah*, was fully consumed on the altar, our lives are to be completely given over to Yahweh in full, sacrificial surrender. I know I need God's help to do this, "for we are His workmanship" (Eph. 2:10). And "I am confident of this very thing, that He who began a good work in you will perfect it until the day of Christ Jesus" (Phil. 1:6).

The Fire That Never Goes Out

One remarkable aspect of the burnt offering is that the fire on the altar was never to go out. Leviticus 6:12 says, "The fire on the altar shall be kept burning on it. *It shall not go out*, but the priest shall burn wood on it every morning." And what was continually placed on the altar? The burnt offering—the *olah*.

Leviticus 1:4 tells us that when the worshipper brought the burnt offering, he was to lay his hand on its head as it was given over to God, "that it may be accepted for him to make atonement on his behalf." This act symbolized that the worshipper was identifying with his offering, making himself one with it. The offering became an extension of the worshipper's soul. And as the sacrifice was burned up in smoke as a fragrant and pleasing aroma to the Lord, the Israelite looked at his own life as being wholly given over to Yahweh.

In this, God is telling us, "When you give yourself over to Me—spirit, soul, mind, and body—My fire will be on the altar to receive you, allowing you to be consumed by My Holy Spirit."

As we saw in the previous chapter, throughout Scripture,

when sacrifices were presented to the Lord, God's manifest presence fell. At the dedication of the Tabernacle, at the inauguration of the Temple, and on numerous other occasions, the people offered sacrifices to Yahweh, and in response, *bam!*—His glory fell. The fire of His Spirit responded to the sacrifice of their surrender.

Beloved, that same fire is burning today. When we yield ourselves to Him completely—not treating Him as a genie to grant our wishes but surrendering to Him on His terms—His Spirit falls and consumes our lives for His glory.

Complete consecration has always been at the center of true worship. Nothing less than our entire devotion will satisfy Him.

Yeshua warned that He will spit the lukewarm out of His mouth (Rev. 3:16). He also declared, "Whoever wishes to save his life will lose it; but whoever loses his life for My sake will find it" (Matt. 16:25). And again, "If anyone wishes to come after Me, he must deny himself, and take up his cross daily and follow Me. For whoever wishes to save his life will lose it, but whoever loses his life for My sake, he is the one who will save it" (Luke 9:23–24).

All these passages point to the same truth: the need to give our lives to Him in total abandonment, total surrender, and total devotion. To follow Jesus, we must give up all our rights and let Him do what He wants with our lives.

The entire *olah* offering being burned unto the Lord as a pleasing aroma is a prophetic picture of what God desires from us: our everything.

So let's ask ourselves: Are our lives totally surrendered to the Lord? Or are there areas we've declared off-limits to Him?

For some of us, it's our eating habits. We're willing to give some parts of our lives to the Lord, but when it comes to food, we're not willing to surrender. For others, it's our emotions, finances, or relationships. This is why God gave Israel the dietary laws of *kashruth*, or kosher laws—because He wanted even the smallest details of their lives sanctified in Him.

Isn't it true that sometimes we compartmentalize our lives? We have all seen believers who seem deeply spiritual in church, quoting Scripture and lifting their hands in worship. But as soon as they leave, everything changes. In the car they erupt in anger at their spouse or children and complain about the message, returning to their "out-of-church" personality. They have one personality with other Christians and a completely different way of being around unbelievers. They become like the world again.

But God is saying, "I've called you for something greater—something far more wonderful than the world can offer. But to receive it, you must give Me your whole life."

Fully Consumed

As we reflect on the prophetic significance of the burnt offering in our lives today, let us also consider this: Leviticus 1:3 reveals that it wasn't just the outside of the sacrifice that got consumed by fire—the innermost parts were also burned up. This powerful image teaches us that God isn't merely looking for outward forms of godliness. He wants us to give Him the secrets of our hearts: our thoughts, motives, and feelings. We must lay down our emotions—our inner life as well as our outer one.

How do we do this? Whenever we find ourselves thinking

a wrong thought—whether it comes from pride, lust, hatred, insecurity, or some other emotion—we need to turn it over to the Lord immediately. We can say, "Father, I realize this thought is not pure. It's not from You. Cleanse me. I want all of me to be a living sacrifice to You."

We need God to sanctify our inward affections and emotions. For many years I thought that because I believed in God, if I felt strongly about something, it must be from Him. It took me years to realize that God is much bigger than my emotions, and not every feeling—no matter how strong—comes from Him.

How many people end their marriages because they no longer feel "in love"? They fall for someone else and convince themselves, "This must be God." But Scripture warns us that we can have *inordinate affections*—feelings we may have in the natural that aren't from God. My heart is not to judge or condemn anyone, but think for a moment about the devastation divorce causes: broken homes, wounded children, and destroyed lives.

Please hear my heart: It's not my intent to make anyone feel guilty. I'm just communicating the truth of God's Word: that we are not to be led by our emotions. Feelings can deceive us. The prophet Jeremiah declared, "The heart is deceitful above all things, and desperately wicked: who can know it?" (Jer. 17:9, KJV).

Beloved, we need to deal with the inner issues of our hearts. In Luke 9, when a man told Yeshua, "I will follow You wherever You go…[but] permit me first to go and bury my father," that was a natural, human response. But what did Jesus say? "Allow the dead to bury their own dead; but as for you, go and proclaim everywhere the kingdom of God" (vv. 57–60). And He added, "No one, after putting his hand to the plow and looking back, is fit for the kingdom of God" (v. 62).

The gospel message we hear preached today is often incomplete because it lacks this concept of total sacrifice. We reduce the message of salvation to saying a quick sinner's prayer, asking people to repeat words such as "Lord Jesus, forgive me. I'm a sinner. Come into my life and take me to heaven." But Yeshua didn't call people to simply repeat a prayer. Instead, He said, "If anyone wishes to come after Me, he must deny himself, and take up his cross daily and follow Me" (Luke 9:23). And, "Whoever wishes to save his life will lose it, but whoever loses his life for My sake and the gospel's will save it" (Mark 8:35).

Will we open our hearts and let the Holy Spirit speak to us? Will we surrender all to Him?

Bringing Him Our Best

As we close this chapter on the burnt offering, let's return once more to Leviticus 1. Notice that God gave His people options when presenting this sacrifice. Verses 6–9 speak of offering a bull. Verses 10–13 describe bringing a sheep or goat. And in verses 14–17, we see that even a pigeon or turtledove could be given.

Why the different options? Because not everyone could afford a bull. Some could bring only a sheep or goat, while others had only a small bird to offer. The key principle is this: *God calls each of us to bring Him our best.*

If a person was wealthy enough to offer a bull but instead

brought a pigeon, their sacrifice would not be acceptable to God because it would reveal a heart unwilling to give everything to Him. But if someone with little brought even the smallest pigeon, their offering would be precious in God's sight because it represented their all.

We see this same principle in the Brit Hadashah (New Testament). In Mark 12, Yeshua watched as people gave at the Temple treasury. Many rich people gave large sums, but then a poor widow came and placed two small copper coins, worth only about a penny today. Calling His disciples to Him, Yeshua said, "Truly I say to you, this poor widow put in more than all the contributors to the treasury; for they all put in out of their surplus, but she, out of her poverty, put in all she owned, all she had to live on" (vv. 43–44).

Think about what Yeshua did for us. As Paul writes in Philippians 2:8, "He humbled Himself by becoming obedient to the point of death, even death on a cross." God is calling us to give that same type of radical love back to Him—an obedience and surrender that hold nothing back.

God is looking for our everything—whatever that may be. There is no other way to walk in faith except to radically give our lives over to Him. That's what the burnt offering is all about. Nothing else will satisfy Him.

Paul said, "To live is Christ and to die is gain" (Phil. 1:21). Just as the fire was always burning on the altar, ready to receive the burnt offering, so the Lord stands ready to receive us—when we come fully committed and wholly abandoned to Him.

Even as the *olah* was totally consumed by Yahweh at the altar of burnt offering, so too the Lord is looking for our all—our total surrender. He is worthy of nothing less.

Chapter 12

A SACRIFICE OF THANKSGIVING: THE GRAIN OFFERING

THE SECOND TYPE of offering the priests presented in the Tabernacle is the grain offering, also called the meat (KJV) or meal (ASV) offering.

We read about this sacrifice in the second chapter of Leviticus:

> Now when anyone presents a grain offering as an offering to the LORD, his offering shall be of fine flour, and he shall pour oil on it and put frankincense on it. He shall then bring it to Aaron's sons the priests; and shall take from it his handful of its fine flour and of its oil with all of its frankincense. And the priest shall offer it up in smoke as its memorial portion on the altar, an offering by fire of a soothing aroma to the LORD.
>
> —LEVITICUS 2:1–2

This offering is known in Hebrew as the *minchah* offering. It was a gift offering, a sacrifice of thanksgiving usually brought along with the burnt offering. God didn't command the people to bring this offering—it was voluntary, which is what made it so special.

Unlike sacrifices made to atone for sin, the grain offering was not about making things right with God; it was about delighting in Him. It was an offering of love, given not out of obligation but out of a desire to honor the One who supplies our every need.

Sometimes the most precious gifts aren't those you receive on your birthday, Christmas, or Hanukkah, but they're the ones you're not expecting—the ones given as a token of a person's appreciation for who you are or what you've done for them. That's the kind of offering this was.

The grain offering shows us that worship isn't just a list of dos and don'ts; it's about offering our love to God freely—from a heart overflowing with gratitude. Just as the Israelites presented fine flour, oil, and frankincense as a *minchah* offering to Yahweh, we too are invited to bring our offerings of love and thanksgiving to the Lord.

But what made these specific elements so significant? What do fine flour, oil, and frankincense reveal about the kind of worship that pleases God?

Fine Flour, Oil, and Frankincense

The gift offering—also known as the meat, meal, or grain offering—was specifically to consist of fine flour, oil, and frankincense.

We must realize that to the ancient Israelites wandering in the wilderness, all three of these ingredients were very costly. Today we can go to the grocery store and easily buy flour, so we don't think of it as a precious commodity. But if we were in the wilderness, it would be a significant sacrifice to offer fine flour, oil, and frankincense.

Remember, David said, "I will not give to the Lord that which costs me nothing." The Lord sees through the outward behavior to the heart, and He wants us to give Him what is precious to us—our best.

The Lord stipulated which specific ingredients this offering should include:

> Now when anyone presents a grain offering as an offering to the Lord, his offering shall be of *fine flour*, and he shall pour *oil* on it and put *frankincense* on it.
>
> —Leviticus 2:1

Fine flour

Leviticus 2 stipulates that the offering was to be made of *fine* flour. It couldn't consist of everyday flour—the flour had to be very fine. This points to the nature of Yeshua. He had been conformed to the image of God in His humanity. Every part of Him was beautiful. Every part of Him had integrity. His entire nature was fine, precious, and conformed to the image of God.

To offer "fine flour" is to say to the Lord, "I want to lavish my love upon You by presenting this offering that reflects how beautiful and precious You are to me."

Oil

The offering also had to have oil within it. The oil speaks of the Holy Spirit because oil in Scripture is often associated with the Spirit of God.

> Then Samuel took the horn of *oil* and anointed him in the midst of his brothers; and *the Spirit of the Lord* came mightily upon David from that day forward. And Samuel arose and went to Ramah.
>
> —1 Samuel 16:13

As David was anointed with oil, representing the Holy Spirit, our lives as believers should be saturated with God's presence. Our worship, service, and daily walk with God should not be mechanical or routine but empowered by the Spirit. This means that every aspect of our lives should be guided by the Ruach HaKodesh. The more we surrender to Him, the more we will reflect the beauty of Yeshua to the world through the fragrance of His Spirit emanating from our lives.

Frankincense

Notice that the offering *had* to contain frankincense. Frankincense has a distinct and strong aroma. It smells lovely.

Oftentimes in Scripture the Lord uses what is called anthropomorphic language, meaning He expresses concepts to us in our language to help us understand. For example, when the Bible refers to the *finger of God*, it's not talking about God's *literal finger*. God is Spirit.

When we hear that an offering is a fragrant or soothing aroma to the Lord, the point is not that the Lord takes pleasure in smelling our earthly, material scents. Rather, it speaks of how sweet and winsome the offering is to Him. Yeshua's life was "an offering and a sacrifice to God as a fragrant aroma" (Eph. 5:2). The gift offering had frankincense in it as a reflection of Yeshua's beauty. Remember, all these offerings point to Yeshua. They are windows into His person and shadows of His glory.

Consider also that the ancient Israelites didn't have lots of fine flour, oil, and frankincense at their disposal. It cost them something to obtain these ingredients. But they spent the money to purchase them because it was their way of telling Yahweh how important He was to them.

It's like a man who buys his wife a lavish diamond ring. A man who spends large amounts of money on his wife is saying to her, "You're precious to me, and I want to spend all this money on you to let you know how significant and valuable you are to me."

That's the heart of the grain offering. It was a voluntary gift offering given out of love and gratitude.

This reminds me of Luke's account of a woman who brought Yeshua an alabaster vial of perfume.

> And there was a woman in the city who was a sinner; and when she learned that He was reclining at the table in the Pharisee's house, she brought an alabaster vial of perfume, and standing behind Him at His feet, weeping, she began to wet His feet with her tears, and kept wiping them with the hair of her head, and kissing His feet and anointing them with the perfume.
>
> —Luke 7:37–38

Have you and I ever done something for the Lord just because we love Him and want to thank Him—not because we have to but because we want to?

The woman in Luke 7 didn't anoint Jesus' feet with the costly perfume because she had to. She didn't do it out of compulsion.

We learn from the *minchah* offering that true worship isn't just about fulfilling a religious duty—it's about offering our love to God freely, from a heart overflowing with gratitude, "not grudgingly or under compulsion, for God loves a cheerful giver" (2 Cor. 9:7).

Beware of Leaven and Honey

Just as God was specific about what to include in the *minchah* offering, He was also clear about what should not be present. We read in Leviticus 2:11 that two ingredients were not to be part of the offering: leaven and honey.

> No grain offering, which you bring to the Lord, shall be made with *leaven*, for you shall not offer up in smoke any leaven or any *honey* as an offering by fire to the Lord.
>
> —Leviticus 2:11

Leaven

In Scripture, leaven is often symbolic of sin, arrogance, and pride. In this instance leaven represents that which is not of God. As leaven permeates and transforms dough, so too can sin infiltrate and corrupt the believer's whole life if left unchecked. We are called to root everything out of our hearts that offends or displeases the Lord.

Honey

The Lord also stated in Leviticus 2:11 that no honey should be in the offering. I believe there are a couple of reasons for this.

Honey was used by pagans in the ancient Middle East as an offering to their deities, trying to bribe and manipulate them, thinking, "If we offer up this sweet substance to our deity, maybe we can twist his arm into doing something good for us," or "Perhaps if we offer this sweet honey to him, it will placate him, and he won't do something bad to us." God is saying to us, "I don't want you offering up honey to Me, trying to manipulate Me as you do your children when you give them candy so they'll be good. I don't need your honey to do good. I'm always good."

The omission of honey in the offering also symbolizes the need to have our physical urges under control. Honey tantalizes and excites the flesh by its sweetness. But "flesh and blood cannot inherit the kingdom of God; nor does the perishable inherit the imperishable" (1 Cor. 15:50). God is accessed only by the spirit. Thus, honey, which inflames the passion of the flesh, is omitted.

I have been in worship services where the leader is trying to get everyone all worked up through fleshly antics. Similarly, we can seek to access God by doing something in the power of our flesh rather than just opening up and drinking of His Spirit. Honey in the offering reflects this propensity of human nature, in hopes of a greater encounter with Him.

The Lord is calling us to offer ourselves as a pure and unaltered sacrifice: free from fleshly striving and the leaven of sin and pride.

A Little Salt

Leviticus 2 goes on to tell us that the grain offering needed to be sprinkled with salt:

> Every grain offering of yours, moreover, you shall *season with salt*, so that the salt of the covenant of your God shall not be lacking from your grain offering; with all your offerings you shall offer salt.
>
> —Leviticus 2:13

Nothing written in that verse is arbitrary. God didn't have to say the offering needed to be sprinkled with salt, but He did, and there's a reason for that.

Salt is a preservative. In the ancient Middle East, the Israelites would put salt on their food to keep it from going bad. So salt being sprinkled on the offerings is Yahweh's way of saying: "This covenant you and I have together will be preserved. Heaven and earth may pass away, but My words shall never pass away."

The Lord wants us to trust Him. As we consider the application of this for our lives today, we must take hold of the fact that the covenant He made with us is *sprinkled with salt*. And He wants us to say: "I trust You, God. You said that You're with me and that You'll never leave me nor forsake me. That's the covenant You made with me, Lord, and I'm going to trust You for that. You said that all authority in heaven and earth is given unto You. I believe that You're sovereign in my life and my circumstances. I believe *the covenant You made with me is sprinkled with salt and that it endures*."

We can know the Word of God, but there is a difference between knowing the Word and trusting the Word. God literally spoke into our world and said, "Sprinkle salt on My offering because I want you to trust Me. I want you to know that the covenant I've established with you will not fade away. Heaven and earth will pass away, but My words will never pass away. I want you to sink your teeth into the unfailing Word of God. Trust Me, for I do not change," says Yahweh. "My purpose is to bless you and keep you, make My face shine upon you, and be gracious to you."

It's also interesting to note that in the ancient Middle East, salt was added to a covenant to seal the friendship. The Lord is saying that the covenant we have with Him is about His friendship with us. (We will talk more about this in the next chapter.)

Lastly, consider before moving on that Yeshua applied this concept about salt to us in a different way. In Matthew 5:13, He said that *we* are the salt of the earth. The concept is similar: We are the ones called to preserve God's presence in the world.

Although we have explored several things about the grain, or *minchah*, offering, at its core it is a love offering. Like the woman of old who anointed Yeshua's feet with a costly bottle of perfume—not out of compulsion but just because she adored Him—let us lavish our love on Him with true devotion.

As we reflect on the grain offering, let's ask ourselves the following: What can I bring to the Lord today—not because I have to but because I want to?

Chapter 13

A REVELATION OF FRIENDSHIP: THE PEACE OFFERING

THE THIRD OFFERING is the peace offering, or *shelamim* in Hebrew. The term comes from the same root as the word *shalom*, which means peace, restoration, wholeness, and completeness.

We read about this offering in the third chapter of Leviticus:

> From the sacrifice of the peace offerings he shall present an offering by fire to the LORD, the fat that covers the entrails and all the fat that is on the entrails, and the two kidneys with the fat that is on them, which is on the loins, and the lobe of the liver, which he shall remove with the kidneys. Then Aaron's sons shall offer it up in smoke on the altar on the burnt offering, which is on the wood that is on the fire; it is an offering by fire of a soothing aroma to the LORD.
>
> —LEVITICUS 3:3–5

The distinguishing feature of the peace offering was that all three parties shared in it: Yahweh Himself (Lev. 3:16), the worshipper who brought the sacrifice (Lev. 7:15–16), and the priest who presented it (Lev. 7:31–34). Scripture even describes it as food.

> Then the priest shall offer it up in smoke on the altar as food, an offering by fire to the LORD.
>
> —LEVITICUS 3:11

The peace offering speaks of friendship and shalom with God. It reminds us that while He is indeed our holy Father—worthy of fear and reverence—He is also our friend, one who draws near and "sticks closer than a brother" (Prov. 18:24).

We see this truth in the life of Enoch. Scripture says, "Enoch walked with God; and he was not, for God took him" (Gen. 5:24). He lived in continual fellowship with the Lord, and his intimacy and friendship with God was so deep that he never even experienced death—God simply drew him into His presence. Enoch shows us that this kind of closeness is possible for human beings who set their hearts on Him.

As a Jewish boy growing up in the synagogue, I don't remember it being communicated to me that God was my friend. I was never told that He cared for me personally or that He could help me with my problems. Then in 1978, Jesus appeared to me in a vision of the night. In time I began reading the New Testament, and there I discovered that God loved me and that He was, in fact, my friend.

I know it may be difficult for some people to believe that the Master of the universe calls us His friends. Yet Yeshua said it plainly: "No longer do I call you slaves, for the slave does not know what his master is doing; but I have called you friends" (John 15:15). And if "the Lord used to speak to Moses face to face, just as a man speaks to his friend" (Exod. 33:11), how much more will He speak to you and me, who have been redeemed by the precious blood of Messiah Jesus?

We Can Touch God's Heart

As I mentioned previously, the Lord, the worshipper, and the priest all consumed a portion of this offering. We read about the Lord's portion in Leviticus 3:16:

> The priest shall offer them up in smoke on the altar as *food*, an offering by fire for a soothing aroma; *all fat is the Lord's.*

The Bible is again using anthropomorphic language by saying this offering was presented to God as food. Obviously, the Lord doesn't eat like we do, but He is using this language to communicate with us in a way we can understand.

Notice in Leviticus 3:16 that it was the fat portion of the offering that belonged to God and was a "soothing aroma" (Lev. 3:5). This language speaks of pleasure. Experiencing a soothing aroma involves delight. In this we see that our friendship brings Him joy.

Beloved, we must understand that we have the ability to touch God emotionally. When we choose to love Him and put Him first, we bring Him pleasure. When we resist or rebel, we grieve Him. It's often difficult to realize this. We assume God is so transcendent, so complete in Himself, that nothing we do could possibly move Him. Yes, He is perfect and whole; we cannot add to or take away from His divinity. Yet somehow you and I—whom He created in His own image to love and fellowship with Him—can either bring Him joy or cause Him pain.

Remember when Yeshua was on earth and Lazarus had died? Lazarus's sister Mary came to Jesus and said, "If You had been here, my brother would not have died" (John 11:32). The Bible says that in response, "Jesus wept" (John 11:35).

> Therefore, when Mary came where Jesus was, she saw Him, and fell at His feet, saying to Him, "Lord, if You had been here, my brother would not have died." When Jesus therefore saw her weeping, and the Jews who came with her also weeping, He was deeply moved in spirit and was troubled, and said, "Where have you laid him?" They said to Him, "Lord, come and see." Jesus wept. So the Jews were saying, "See how He loved him!" But some of them said, "Could not this man, who opened the eyes of the blind man, have kept this man also from dying?"
>
> —John 11:32–37

He was moved—not just intellectually or spiritually but emotionally.

God has emotions like we do. Remember, we were created in His likeness (Gen. 1:27). Do we as humans have emotions? If so, then God must have emotions. Another example of this is that the Bible tells us on more than one occasion that Jesus was moved with compassion (Matt. 20:34; Mark 1:41). Conversely, both the Hebrew Bible and the New Testament inform us that we can grieve God's Spirit (Isa. 63:10; Eph. 4:30). To grieve means to bring sorrow.

This is why the peace offering was so special. When a worshipper came before the Lord with this sacrifice, they were declaring, "I love You." For this reason the Scripture says it rose as a soothing aroma. It brought Him pleasure.

A Marriage Supper

As we've seen, the peace offering was unique in that the Lord, the worshipper, and the priest also consumed a portion of it (Lev. 7). What a picture this paints for us—God, the priest, and the worshipper sharing a meal together. A meal is a symbol of friendship and fellowship.

When I think of the peace offering, I am reminded of Revelation 19:7, 9: "Let us rejoice and be glad and give the glory to Him, for the marriage of the Lamb has come and His bride has made herself ready.…Blessed are those who are invited to the *marriage supper of the Lamb*." The ultimate fulfillment of the peace offering is seen in this marriage supper, where *God and His people will share a meal and celebrate their covenant relationship.* Wow!

Marriage represents the pinnacle of intimacy. On the night before Messiah was crucified, He shared a meal with His disciples that is often referred to as the Last Supper. There He said to them, "I will not drink of this fruit of the vine from now on until that day when I drink it new with you in My Father's kingdom" (Matt. 26:29). That day is the marriage supper of the Lamb.

Beloved, God wants us to understand who He is to us. He is here. He's not a God who is far away. Let's pray for a deeper revelation of this truth. Friendship with God is not just a theological concept to know in our minds; it is something to pray into until it becomes revelation in our hearts.

We need to keep praying until we gain revelation. The reality is that for those of us in relationship with Yahweh, God is our friend. We can grow in our understanding and experience of this by praying about it. Maybe you don't feel all that close to God. Pray. Ask and you'll receive. Seek and you'll find. Pray while driving to work, at work, and at home. Pray continually:

Lord, help me know that You're my friend. Help me know how near You are—even closer than a brother. Help me experience the reality that You're the best friend I could ever have. Help me grab hold of this truth deep inside. Imprint upon my soul the knowledge of Your love for me so I can experience fellowship with You.

The peace offering—the *shelamim*, the offering of shalom—is about completeness. It's about sitting at His table, knowing we belong to Him through Yeshua.

So far we've looked at the first three offerings, the ones that rose up as a sweet aroma to the Lord.

1. The burnt offering (*olah*) reminded us that we must be totally consumed and fully surrendered to Yahweh.
2. The grain offering (*minchah*) showed us the joy of giving to God simply because we love Him and He is worthy.
3. And the peace offering (*shelamim*) revealed the fellowship, friendship, and shalom we have with God through Yeshua.

But not all offerings arose as a pleasing fragrance to God. In the next chapter, we're going to look at the second category of sacrifices: the *sin* and *trespass* offerings. These were not sweet aromas—as sin is never sweet. These offerings remind us that sin is ugly and costly, yet they also reveal the mercy of God, who made a way for us to be cleansed and restored.

Chapter 14

SIN, SACRIFICE, AND MERCY: THE SIN AND TRESPASS OFFERINGS

THE LAST OF the five primary offerings presented in the Tabernacle are the sin (*chattat*) and trespass (*asham*) offerings. Though similar, these two offerings had different purposes.

The sin offering, referenced in Leviticus 4, was for the one who had committed sin. This would include sins committed due to ignorance or without full awareness. It was also for sins committed accidentally.

The trespass offering, on the other hand—outlined in Leviticus 5 and 6—addressed *specific* sins the Israelite had committed. *Also known as the guilt offering*, it was particularly for sins done unintentionally, as seen in the following verses:

> If a person acts unfaithfully and sins *unintentionally* against the Lord's holy things, then he shall bring his guilt [trespass] offering to the LORD: a ram without defect from the flock, according to your valuation in silver by shekels, in terms of the shekel of the sanctuary, for a guilt offering.
>
> —LEVITICUS 5:15

> Now if a person sins and does any of the things which the Lord has commanded not to be done, *though he was unaware*, still he is guilty and shall bear his punishment. He is then to bring to the priest a ram without defect

> from the flock, according to your valuation, for a guilt offering. So the priest shall make atonement for him concerning his error in which he sinned *unintentionally* and did not know it, and it will be forgiven him.
>
> —Leviticus 5:17–18

While trespass (guilt) offerings were generally for sins committed unintentionally, when we study some of the specific sins this offering atones for, we rightly wonder how the sins listed in Leviticus 5 and 6 could have been done unintentionally. For example, we read in chapter 6:

> When a person sins and acts unfaithfully against the Lord, and *deceives* his companion in regard to a deposit or a security entrusted to him, or through *robbery*, or if he has *extorted* from his companion, or has found what was lost and *lied* about it and sworn falsely, so that he sins in regard to any one of the things a man may do…he shall make restitution for it in full and add to it one-fifth more.…Then he shall bring to the priest his guilt offering to the Lord…and the priest shall make atonement for him before the Lord.
>
> —Leviticus 6:2–3, 5–7

How do you deceive someone unintentionally regarding a deposit? How do you rob or extort a person unintentionally? Yet a person could present an offering to atone for these trespasses. How do we explain this? According to rabbinic thought, the discrepancy between the offering being for unintentional sins and the fact that the sins covered include robbery, extortion, lying, and swearing falsely—which seem to clearly indicate intentionality—is explained by repentance.

When the sinner is convicted of his guilt, makes restitution, brings the proper offering, and seeks forgiveness, his sins can be atoned for. Even though they were intentional at the time, because the sinner did not fully understand the gravity of his sin, God showed mercy through the trespass offering.

Remember Yeshua on the cross? His accusers plucked out His beard. Was that intentional? I would say so. They spit on Him and jeered at Him. Was that intentional? I would say so. And yet as He looked upon those who reviled Him, Yeshua said, "Father, forgive them, for they know not what they do" (Luke 23:34, MEV). If they didn't know what they were doing, that suggests their sin was unintentional. But the soldiers and onlookers didn't pluck out His beard or spit on Him accidentally, so why would Yeshua say their abuse was unintentional?

Because they didn't have revelation. I believe that's how we are to understand the trespass offering. It atoned for sins people committed without having the revelation of the Holy Spirit to fully understand the gravity of their actions, when they didn't realize they were rebelling against the ways of God.

The Unpardonable Sin

This distinction helps us understand Jesus' words about blaspheming the Holy Spirit in Matthew 12. The Scripture says, "Any sin and blasphemy shall be forgiven people, but blasphemy against the Spirit shall not be forgiven. Whoever speaks a word against the Son of Man, it shall be forgiven him; but whoever speaks against the Holy Spirit, it shall not be forgiven him, either in this age or in the age to come" (Matt. 12:31–32).

I remember reading those verses as a young believer and being terrified of blaspheming the Holy Spirit. The thought of sinning in this way paralyzed me until the Lord set me free. In time I came to see what made this sin different from others and to understand that we must look at the verse in its broader context.

> Then a demon-possessed man who was blind and mute was brought to Jesus, and He healed him, so that the mute man spoke and saw....But when the Pharisees heard this, they said, "This man casts out demons only by Beelzebul the ruler of the demons."
>
> And knowing their thoughts Jesus said to them, "...If Satan casts out Satan, he is divided against himself; how then will his kingdom stand? If I by Beelzebul cast out demons, by whom do your sons cast them out?...But if I cast out demons by the Spirit of God, then the kingdom of God has come upon you....He who is not with Me is against Me; and he who does not gather with Me scatters.
>
> "Therefore I say to you, any sin and blasphemy shall be forgiven people, but blasphemy against the Spirit shall not be forgiven. Whoever speaks a word against the Son of Man, it shall be forgiven him; but whoever speaks against the Holy Spirit, it shall not be forgiven him, either in this age or in the age to come."
>
> —MATTHEW 12:22, 24–28, 30–32

In this passage, Yeshua drove demons out of someone by the Spirit of God, and the religious leaders accused Him of casting out the demons by the devil. Yeshua told them, "If I cast out demons by the Spirit of God, know that the kingdom of God has come upon you." And then He said in essence, "If you speak a word against Me, you can be forgiven, but if you speak a word against the Holy Spirit, you can never be forgiven, in this age or the age to come."

We know people can be forgiven for speaking against Jesus because when He was on the cross, His accusers mocked Him, spit on Him, and jeered at Him, and yet Yeshua said, "Father, *forgive them; for they do not know what they are doing*" (Luke 23:34). It's the same thing that took place in Leviticus chapters 5 and 6. Lying, plucking out Messiah Jesus' beard, hitting and mocking Him—it all seemed to be very intentional. But Yeshua said they didn't have revelation. They really didn't know who He was. However, when someone knows the truth because the power of the Holy Spirit has made it known to them—when deep inside they have an inner witness of the truth and choose to harden their hearts defiantly and reject the Holy Spirit—then they sever themselves from their only hope of salvation and forgiveness.

In Leviticus 5 and 6, the person was sinning, but they were doing it in spiritual ignorance. The apostle Paul once persecuted Christians and even participated in the stoning of Stephen (Acts 7). But Paul said, "I was formerly a blasphemer and a persecutor and a violent aggressor. Yet I was shown mercy *because I acted ignorantly in unbelief*; and the grace of our Lord was more than abundant, with the faith and love which are found in Christ Jesus" (1 Tim. 1:13–14).

Paul was acting in ignorance, and God showed him mercy. But when God has made the truth known to someone and they keep hardening their hearts against it, they sever themselves from the grace of God forever. The Bible says, "If we go on sinning willfully after receiving the knowledge of the truth, there no longer remains a sacrifice for sins, but a terrifying expectation of judgment and the fury of a fire which will consume the adversaries" (Heb. 10:26–27).

There comes a time when the Holy Spirit makes the truth known to an individual. They didn't just hear it, and they didn't just read about it, but the Holy Spirit Himself bore witness with their heart to the truth. At that point, the person has an opportunity to open their heart and surrender to the truth or to rebelliously harden their heart. When they do the latter, they're blaspheming the Holy Spirit—they're rejecting Yeshua after the Holy Spirit has clearly revealed Him to them.

This is often a process that happens over time, but at some point the Holy Spirit says, "This is as far as I can go with you. This is your last chance. If you harden your heart to this gospel truth now, I'm going to leave, and there's nothing left for you but a fearful expectation of judgment."

Don't Harden Your Heart

Beloved, has God been speaking to you over and over about something, yet you still haven't repented? When presenting the sin and trespass offerings, not only was it necessary for the Israelite to bring the offering, but it was also necessary for them to repent. The sinner had to turn away from the sin. They had to change.

If the Holy Spirit has been bearing witness with your spirit about repenting, don't harden your heart defiantly so that He leaves you and there is no longer a sacrifice for your sin but only a fearful expectation of judgment. The Bible says, "Today if you hear His voice, do not harden your hearts" (Heb. 3:7).

God will not strive with you forever (Gen. 6:3). Numbers 15:30–31 says:

> But the person who does anything defiantly, whether he is native or an alien, that one is blaspheming the LORD; and that person shall be cut off from among his people. Because he has despised the word of the LORD and has broken His commandment, that person shall be completely cut off; his guilt will be on him.

Remember, we read in Leviticus 5 and 6 that an offering could be given for the one who lacks revelation and sins unintentionally. But when a person has revelation and sins out of rebellion, that's when they're in danger of blaspheming the Spirit of God because they're deliberately telling Him no when they know He's saying yes to them.

Numbers 15:30 says, "The person who does anything *defiantly*." This is the difference. The behavior is knowingly defiant. It's rebellious.

Yeshua told the religious leaders in Matthew 12 that they could say something against Him and be forgiven. Maybe, not knowing any better, they thought He was just a man and not the Son of God, or perhaps they thought He was a crazy liar. That could be forgiven. But Yeshua was telling us in Matthew 12 that when the Holy Spirit makes Himself known to you and you *defiantly* rebel, you're blaspheming the Holy Spirit, and that sin cannot be atoned.

Look once again at Numbers 15:30–31:

> The person who does anything *defiantly*, whether he is native or an alien, that one is blaspheming the Lord; and that person shall be cut off from among his people....That person shall be completely cut off; his guilt will be on him.

Notice how strikingly similar the language is to Yeshua's words about blaspheming the Holy Spirit:

> Therefore I say to you, any sin and blasphemy shall be forgiven people, but blasphemy against the Spirit shall not be forgiven. Whoever speaks a word against the Son of Man, it shall be forgiven him; but whoever speaks against the Holy Spirit, it shall not be forgiven him, either in this age or in the age to come.
>
> —Matthew 12:31–32

In Numbers 15, the Lord tells us that a person who sins defiantly shall be cut off from among his people. This, again, is much like what we read in the Book of Hebrews:

> For if we go on sinning *willfully* after receiving the knowledge of the truth, there no longer remains a sacrifice for sins, but a terrifying expectation of judgment and the fury of a fire which will consume the adversaries.
>
> —Hebrews 10:26–27

Paid with Blood

The sin and trespass offerings always involved the shedding of blood:

> Then the anointed priest is to take some of the *blood* of the bull and bring it to the tent of meeting, and the priest shall dip his finger in the *blood* and sprinkle some of

> the *blood* seven times before the LORD, in front of the veil of the sanctuary. The priest shall also put some of the *blood* on the horns of the altar of fragrant incense which is before the LORD in the tent of meeting; and all the *blood* of the bull he shall pour out at the base of the altar of burnt offering which is at the doorway of the tent of meeting.
>
> —LEVITICUS 4:5–7

> He shall also sprinkle some of the *blood* of the sin offering on the side of the altar, while the rest of the *blood* shall be drained out at the base of the altar: it is a sin offering.
>
> —LEVITICUS 5:9

Why is this? Because Yahweh said in Leviticus 17:11, "The life of the flesh is in the blood, and I have given it to you on the altar to make atonement for your souls; for it is the blood by reason of the life that makes atonement." That's what these two offerings were—offerings of atonement.

Some people think the crown of the human being is their mind and that their identity is found in their ability to think and reason. Others believe the primary seat of an individual's life force is in the heart. But the Lord tells us in His Word that the life of the flesh is not in the mind or the heart; it's in the blood. Blood carries nutrients, fights infection, distributes hormones, transports oxygen, and removes waste. Blood is our lifeforce and is sacred. There is a mystery in this. That's why on Yom Kippur, the high priest would bring the blood of the bull and the goat inside the Holy of Holies and pour it on the altar over the Ark of the Covenant.

Before I close, I want to make a final comment about the sin and the trespass offerings. As I said earlier, it wasn't enough to bring an offering but then continue to sin. The worshipper also needed to repent. We read in Leviticus 5:16, "He shall make restitution for that which he has sinned against the holy thing." Of course, this is prophetic, because not only do we need to come to Jesus, but we need to repent. We need to turn to Him. There must be a change. We can't just keep coming to Him asking for forgiveness without repentance. That's why Yeshua said in Luke 13:3, "Unless you repent, you will all likewise perish."

Through the sacrifices offered in the Tabernacle, we learn that God is not looking for the cheap form of Christianity we so often hear preached today. Oftentimes the message being taught is not the gospel of Scripture—the gospel seen in the five offerings Yahweh commanded the Israelites to bring to Him in the Tabernacle.

The modern gospel prioritizes our needs and comfort. But the true gospel calls us to surrender our lives fully to Yahweh, holding nothing back, as we see modeled in the burnt offering. It challenges us to come before the Lord, thanking Him—not because He has fulfilled our wish list but just because we love Him, like the Israelites did when they brought the Lord the *minchah*, or grain, offering. It reminds us that God is our friend and wants to have fellowship with us, as we see reflected in the *shelamim*, the peace offering. And it challenges us to repent of our sin, turn from it completely, and allow the Lord to make us more and more like Him, as He did for the ancient Israelites when they brought Him their sin (*chattat*) and trespass (*asham*) offerings.

Beloved, this is the lifestyle that leads us to intimacy with God. This is the depth of fellowship the Lord wants to draw us into through the blueprint of the Tabernacle. In the next chapter, we will see how Yeshua fulfilled all these offerings when He sacrificed His life for you and me once and for all. Every detail in the Tabernacle, every sacrifice—it's all about Jesus!

Chapter 15

JESUS—THE AUTHOR OF A NEW COVENANT

WE'VE BEEN LOOKING at the five primary sacrifices offered up to Yahweh in the Tabernacle. The Lord called His people to bring these offerings to Him because, in doing so, they were brought close to Him. That's what *korban,* the Hebrew word often translated "sacrifice," means—to draw near. Yet we must understand that these offerings were all fulfilled in Messiah Yeshua. They all point to Him because He alone is the final solution.

At times we may not truly know who Jesus is for us. We think our salvation lies in Yeshua plus something—Yeshua plus our works. Although we may not think we look to something other than Yeshua to be acceptable to God, if we really examine our thought processes, we may find that we do. On the one hand, we believe we're saved by the grace of God. Yet on the other, we're afraid that if we don't pray for a certain length of time, read our Bible long enough, attend church each week, and all the other things we might measure our spiritual state by, we might not be saved.

The reality is that if we are saved, the Holy Spirit is in us, and He's going to produce His fruit in our lives. Jesus said, "I am the vine, you are the branches; he who abides in Me and I in him, he bears much fruit, for apart from Me you can do nothing" (John 15:5). We are not saved by our works. We're saved by Yeshua alone.

Messiah Yeshua is the fulfillment of all the sacrifices we've examined—and if we have Him, we have everything. This is revealed to us most clearly in the Book of Hebrews.

> Now the main point in what has been said is this: we have such a high priest, who has taken His seat at the right hand of the throne of the Majesty in the heavens, a minister in the sanctuary and in the true tabernacle, which the Lord pitched, not man. For every high priest is appointed to offer both gifts and sacrifices; so it is necessary that this high priest also have something to offer.
>
> —HEBREWS 8:1–3

Yeshua had something to offer. He didn't bring with Him a burnt offering consisting of an animal or a grain offering made of fine flour, oil, and frankincense. What Yeshua brought was the offering of Ephesians 5—Himself, as He "gave Himself up for us, an offering and a sacrifice to God as a fragrant aroma" (Eph. 5:2).

Hebrews 8 continues:

> But now He has obtained a more excellent ministry, by as much as He is also the mediator of a better covenant, which has been enacted on better promises. For if that first covenant had been faultless, there would have been no occasion sought for a second.
>
> —HEBREWS 8:6–7

Yeshua Himself has come, and He has brought a better covenant. It's important that you don't mix the Law and your works with Messiah Yeshua. The Law has a purpose, which I discuss at length in my book *Decoding the Torah*. But it's fundamentally important that you don't view your salvation as dependent on Yeshua plus the Law. It's Jesus alone who saves you. The covenant the Lord inaugurated in Yeshua is complete. We read in Hebrews 8:8–9:

> Behold, days are coming, says the Lord, when I will effect a new covenant with the house of Israel and with the house of Judah; not like the covenant which I made with their fathers on the day when I took them by the hand to lead them out of the land of Egypt; for they did not continue in My covenant, and I did not care for them, says the Lord.

The Lord goes on to say in verse 13 that the Mosaic covenant has become obsolete in terms of fulfilling the purpose it once served. We're no longer made right with God by keeping the Mosaic covenant. We're made right with Him through Messiah Yeshua.

Romans 7 tells us that before Yeshua came, those who were in covenant with God were married to the Law.

> Or do you not know, brethren (for I am speaking to those who know the law), that the law has jurisdiction over a person as long as he lives? For the married woman is bound by law to her husband while he is living; but if her husband dies, she is released from the law concerning the husband. So then, if while her husband is living she is joined to another man, she shall be called an adulteress; but if her husband dies, she is free from the law, so that she is not an adulteress though she is joined to another man. Therefore, my brethren, you also were made to die to the Law through the body of Christ, so that you might be joined to another, to Him who was raised from the dead, in order that we might bear fruit for God.
>
> —Romans 7:1–4

In this passage the apostle Paul compared the relationship we have with the Law to a woman who is bound to her husband in marriage as long as he is living. If she were to begin a relationship with another man while her husband was alive, she'd be in adultery. But if her husband died, she would be free to marry another man.

This is what the Lord is telling us about our relationship with the Law. Before Yeshua came, we were married to the Law. But through His death, resurrection, and ascension, Messiah Jesus inaugurated a better way to be in covenant with God. We were released from the Law to be joined to Father God through Yeshua.

Beloved, it's all about Jesus—and it's *only* about Jesus. He's the Lamb sitting on the throne, and when we get to heaven, we're going to give Him glory and honor forever and ever. We won't be worshipping the Lamb plus our works. We won't be praising the Lamb plus our own righteousness. We won't be giving honor to the Lamb plus our religious activities. We're going to only be worshipping the Lamb.

Partakers of a New Covenant

Hebrews 8 goes on to say in verse 13:

> When He said, "A new covenant," He has made the first obsolete. But whatever is becoming obsolete and growing old is ready to disappear.

What is this verse telling us? The apostle Paul writes in the Book of Romans that Yeshua's coming was witnessed by the

Law and the Prophets, but He came apart from the Law and the Prophets.

> But now apart from the Law the righteousness of God has been manifested, being witnessed by the Law and the Prophets, even the righteousness of God through faith in Jesus Christ for all those who believe; for there is no distinction; for all have sinned and fall short of the glory of God, being justified as a gift by His grace through the redemption which is in Christ Jesus; whom God displayed publicly as a propitiation in His blood through faith. This was to demonstrate His righteousness, because in the forbearance of God He passed over the sins previously committed; for the demonstration, I say, of His righteousness at the present time, so that He would be just and the justifier of the one who has faith in Jesus.
>
> —Romans 3:21–26

In other words, we are saved by a righteousness that's not connected to the Law and the Prophets. Rather, we are saved only by the righteousness that was witnessed, or attested to, by the Law and the Prophets. Simply put, Jesus came apart from the Law and the Prophets, and He alone saves us.

The teaching of the Law is valuable when you don't approach it legalistically or as something that can help you earn righteousness. The Law is a revelation of God's nature, but we don't look at Jesus through the Law. We look at the Law through Jesus. There's a big difference.

Yeshua said, "I am the way, and the truth, and the life; no one comes to the Father but through Me" (John 14:6). Beloved, make your faith all about Messiah Yeshua. Don't get distracted and search endlessly for Him in books and popular teachers.

Jesus said to the Pharisees, "You search the Scriptures because you think that in them you have eternal life; it is these that testify about Me; and you are unwilling to come to Me so that you may have life" (John 5:39–40). Life is found in Jesus, for "He who has the Son has life" (1 John 5:12, NKJV).

Keep your eyes fixed on Jesus, and you won't be led astray. If you have accepted Yeshua and are His, "you have an anointing from the Holy One" (1 John 2:20), and the Spirit of God "will guide you into all the truth; for He will not speak on His own initiative, but whatever He hears, He will speak; and He will disclose to you what is to come" (John 16:13).

We read in Hebrews, "He entered the holy place once for all, having obtained eternal redemption" (Heb. 9:12). Messiah Jesus has come. He is the author and finisher of our faith. We must continually fix our eyes on Yeshua and seek Him alone.

I believe we should look for the spiritual application of the Mosaic Law because Romans 7:12 says the Law is "holy and righteous and good." But it never takes the place of Jesus. He is the lens we're looking through when we consider the Law.

Yeshua declares in Hebrews 10:9, "Behold, I have come to do Your will." Then the writer says, "He [Messiah] takes away the first in order to establish the second." Messiah Jesus replaced the Mosaic Law with a new and better covenant.

Now please don't misunderstand. Scripture needs to be interpreted with Scripture. Jesus said, "Do not think that I came to abolish the Law or the Prophets; I did not come to abolish but to fulfill" (Matt. 5:17). I love the Torah and the Mosaic Law and believe every believer should be equipped and trained in righteousness by it.

> All Scripture is inspired by God and profitable for teaching, for reproof, for correction, for training in righteousness; so that the man of God may be adequate, equipped for every good work.
>
> —2 Timothy 3:16–17

But as followers of Yeshua, we are no longer seeking to gain access to the Lord through the Mosaic Law. We are released from that system, as Romans 7 says, to be married to the Lord through Messiah Jesus.

That's what the writer of Hebrews means when he says He takes away the first in order to establish the second. I encourage you to read Romans 7 in its entirety so you can see more fully what Hebrews 10:9 is telling us.

It Is Finished

Continuing in Hebrews 10, we read in verses 11–12:

> Every priest stands daily ministering and offering time after time the same sacrifices, which can never take away sins; but He, having offered one sacrifice for sins for all time, sat down at the right hand of God.

Verse 11 says the priests in the Tabernacle stood daily. When you're standing, the work isn't done. But what did Jesus do after He offered Himself as a living sacrifice? He sat down at the right hand of God.

Under the old covenant, the work was never done. That's why the priest was standing. The blood of bulls and goats could never take away sin, "but *He*, having offered one sacrifice for sins for all time, *sat down* at the right hand of God."

Yeshua sat down because the work was finished. Jesus' death on the cross paid the penalty for all our sins: past, present, and future. That doesn't mean we're not called to repent; we saw in the last chapter that we must repent and turn from our sins: the wrong choices, bad attitudes, and harmful behaviors that separate us from God.

When Jesus died on the cross two thousand years ago, you and I hadn't been born, and our sins were yet to be committed. The point is that Yeshua's blood covers all our sin.

Imagine yourself standing under a waterfall of Jesus' blood forever. Envision the pure, beautiful blood of Jesus constantly being poured over you, cleansing you for eternity.

Before we move on, I want to look at one last passage in Hebrews 10:

> For by one offering He has perfected for all time those who are sanctified.…Now where there is forgiveness of these things, there is no longer any offering for sin. Therefore, brethren, since we have confidence to enter the holy place by the blood of Jesus…let us draw near with a sincere heart in full assurance of faith, having our hearts sprinkled clean from an evil conscience and our bodies washed with pure water.
>
> —HEBREWS 10:14, 18–19, 22

Remember, the priest in the Tabernacle had to offer the same sacrifices year after year. But once you come into a relationship with the Lord through Jesus, your sins are forgiven for all time. His one offering has perfected for all time those who are His. "Where there is forgiveness of these things, there is no longer any offering for sin" (v. 18). It's done. Messiah sat down, and we can now "have confidence to enter the holy place by the blood of Jesus" (v. 19).

There is now no condemnation for those who have come to God through His Son, Jesus (Rom. 8:1–2). The blood of Yeshua is sufficient to cleanse whatever we've done in the past. If the Lord took out the penalty for your sin on Jesus, He has no interest in taking it out on you too. When Yeshua died on the cross, they spit on Him, laughed at Him, and pierced His side. The Father turned His face away, causing Him to cry out, "'Eli, Eli, lama sabachthani?' that is, 'My God, My God, why have You forsaken Me?'" (Matt. 27:46). When Jesus descended into the lower parts of the earth, where hell is, He experienced the penalty for our sins. And now that the Lord has taken out the punishment for our sin on His Son, He's not going to take it out on us too. Father God wants you and me to come to Him boldly and pour out our hearts to Him.

Don't Look Back

Let me tell you, there's nothing God doesn't know about you. There's nothing you can tell Him—nothing you've thought or spoken—that will shock Him. There's no part of your life that God isn't fully aware of, so stop hiding. Don't let the devil keep you buried in shame. The blood and sacrifice of Jesus have made final atonement of your sin, and Yeshua has purged you. Our only response now is to have confidence in that truth and develop intimacy with God, fully assured that we're loved, accepted, and received by Him.

So many believers are still living in shame over past sexual sins. If that's you, the Lord doesn't want you to hold on to that condemnation any longer. Remember the woman caught in adultery in John 8? The religious teachers and Pharisees wanted to stone her to death. But Jesus said to them, "He who is without sin among you, let him be the first to throw a stone at her" (v. 7). Then He stooped down and wrote on the ground. After that, all the woman's accusers walked away, and Yeshua said, "'Woman, where are they? Did no one condemn you?' She said, 'No one, Lord.' And Jesus said, '*I do not condemn you, either. Go. From now on sin no more*'" (vv. 10–11).

If you are living under condemnation and shame for past sins, I want you to know God releases you from that. Just live for Him now. Just love Him now. We do have to repent. After Jesus healed the lame man at the pool of Bethesda, He told him, "Behold, you have become well; do not sin anymore, so that nothing worse happens to you" (John 5:14). We don't have to be defined by the past.

Whatever you've done, God forgives you. You can't change the past. So, like Paul, forget what lies behind and look forward to what lies ahead, reaching toward the upward call of God in Messiah Yeshua (Phil. 3:12–14). Stop allowing the devil to make you look back with regret and shame.

My prayer is that we would know, deep in our hearts, that we are complete in Messiah Jesus. In Yeshua, not only are our sins forgiven, but we have been made priests unto God (Rev. 5:10). This isn't merely a title—it's our true identity. Knowing our identity changes how we live, how we see ourselves, and how we relate to our Maker. In the chapters ahead, we are going to discover how the garments of the high priest of Israel reveal our new identity in Messiah—an identity marked by holiness, glory, and beauty.

Part III

THE PRIESTHOOD OF BELIEVERS

Chapter 16

A NEW SPIRITUAL IDENTITY

OUR STUDY OF the Tabernacle now takes us to the highly significant—and highly symbolic—garb of the high priest and its prophetic application for our lives today.

As we start our journey, we're going all the way back to the very beginning, to the Book of Bereshit (Genesis). In chapter 1, verse 27, we read: "God created man in His own image, in the image of God He created him; male and female He created them." This is talking about our original state before Adam and Eve disobeyed God and sin entered the world.

Genesis 2:25 tells us that "the man and his wife were both naked and were not ashamed." But immediately after Adam and Eve ate of the tree of the knowledge of good and evil—the tree the Lord had warned them not to eat from—their eyes were opened, and they suddenly realized they were naked. It was as if some type of covering had been removed from them. They had been naked before the fall too, but now they *felt* naked. Genesis 3:7 says, "They knew that they were naked; and they sewed fig leaves together and made themselves loin coverings."

Before the fall, Adam and Eve were wearing the clothing of the Spirit of God over their flesh. They were not flesh-conscious; they were Spirit-conscious. They were not defined by their flesh; they were defined by their identity in God's Spirit. This is why they were both naked and yet not ashamed. They didn't feel uncovered because they were wearing the clothing of God's Holy Spirit.

But as soon as they ate of the tree, they experienced exactly what the Creator said would happen. They fell out of the Spirit's covering and Holy Spirit–consciousness. They now had a flesh-conscious mindset because the Spirit was gone.

Through Messiah Jesus, God made a way for us to reclaim what was lost in the garden. But we first need to understand what we once had.

Three Attributes of God

Most believers know we were made in God's image, but few really know what that means. We've heard, for example, that God thinks, feels, loves, and has a will, and as human beings we also think, feel, love, and have a will. But there is more to it than having a mind and a will like He does. To truly understand what it means to be made in the image of God, we must consider what characteristics God possesses. You and I were created with those same qualities.

The trait that defines God more than anything else is His holiness. We read in Revelation 4 that when John looked into heaven, he saw the Lord seated on His throne. And around the throne were four living creatures who never stopped crying out day and night, "Holy, holy, holy is the Lord God, the Almighty, who was and who is and who is to come" (v. 8).

The *Tanakh (the* Hebrew Bible) tells us the same thing in Isaiah 6. The prophet had a vision of the Lord and saw Him high and lifted up, exalted on a throne. And there were holy beings around God's throne, saying day and night, "Holy,

Holy, Holy, is the LORD of hosts, the whole earth is full of His glory" (v. 3).

God's holiness means He's utterly unique, utterly set apart, and utterly different. That's how He made you and me unlike anything else in His creation. When you understand that you have been created in God's image, let me tell you, it will cause you to think something of yourself. It will give you a holy and sacred self-respect. It will cause you to realize that, like David, you are "fearfully and wonderfully made" (Ps. 139:14).

Another trait that stands out when I think of the Lord is His glory. The Hebrew word *kavod* refers to the weight of His glory. God is preeminent in glory, and if He created man in His own image, He has also created you and me for glory.

In Exodus 15, God had just supernaturally parted the Red Sea and delivered the Israelites from Egypt. After they reached the other side and the Lord drowned their enemies in the sea, the children of Israel sang this song: "Who is like You, O LORD, among the gods? Who is like You, glorious in holiness, fearful in praises, doing wonders?" (v. 11, NKJV). Our God is *glorious*. He is clothed in majesty, and the earth is filled with His glory.

Before the fall, when Adam and Eve were in the Garden of Eden, they felt the glory of God on them because they were created in His image. God wants us to again live in the reality that His glory is upon our lives.

I could go on listing the qualities of God, but I want to talk about just one more trait that Adam and Eve were clothed with before the fall. It's an attribute we don't think about often enough: God's beauty.

We think a lot about the power of God, and we think of God as all-knowing. But we don't think enough about His beauty. Yet the Bible tells us in Romans:

> That which is known about God is evident within them; for God made it evident to them. For since the creation of the world His invisible attributes, His eternal power and divine nature, have been clearly seen, being understood through what has been made.
>
> —Romans 1:19–20

Paul is teaching us here that creation reveals who God is. When we behold the deep blue of the sky, the lush green of the grass, and the majesty of the trees, we are seeing God's beauty. His beauty is everywhere—in the mountains that tower above us, in the oceans that roar with power, in the rivers and waterfalls that flow with grace. It's in the animals roaming in the wild, the birds soaring in the sky, and the butterflies that dance on the wind. When we look at the beauty around us, we realize that someone who made such a beautiful creation would be beautiful Himself.

David said in Psalm 27:4, "One thing I have asked from the Lord, that I shall seek: That I may dwell in the house of the Lord all the days of my life, to *behold the beauty of the Lord* and to meditate in His temple." God is beautiful, and because we were created in His image, we were made to reflect this same beauty.

Again, God is holy, He's clothed in glory, and He's beautiful. These are His three primary characteristics, and they were part of the spiritual clothing Adam and Eve wore in the garden before the fall. Yet when they fell into sin, they no longer felt holiness. They no longer felt glory. They no longer felt beauty. Those spiritual garments had been removed.

But when the Lord redeemed Israel through the blood of the ancient Passover lamb, He made them a *kingdom of priests* (Exod. 19:6). And those of us who have come into relationship with the Lamb of God—Yeshua HaMashiach (Jesus the Messiah)—have also been made "priests to our God" (Rev. 5:10; see also 1 Peter 2:9). When we were redeemed by the blood of the Lamb and brought into this priesthood relationship, God gave us back the clothes of holiness, glory, and beauty that had been lost in the garden.

It is as Yeshua promised His disciples in Luke 24:49: "Behold, I am sending forth the promise of My Father upon you; but you are to stay in the city *until you are clothed with power from on high*." By the power of God's Spirit, we have been clothed once again with garments of holiness, glory, and beauty from heaven on high. Hallelujah!

Our High Priestly Garments

The garments of the high priest described in Exodus 28 reflect this: "You shall make *holy* garments for Aaron your brother, for *glory* and for *beauty*" (v. 2).

First, as priests of God, we have been given holy garments. That means God has set us apart! Not everyone in Israel was wearing the priestly garments—only the high priest wore them. As a priest, you've been called to be unique. That's what holiness means: to be unique and different from the people around you.

Not only were these garments holy, not only were they set

apart, but they were also garments of glory and beauty. Here's the issue: If you're not willing to be different, if you're not willing to be set apart, then you won't experience the glory and beauty that go along with these garments.

Too many of God's people are unwilling to take on the garment of holiness. They're not willing to be unique. They're not willing to be set apart. They just want to fit in and be like everybody else. They're one way when they are worshipping in church, but when they go back into their workplace or to their unsaved family members, no one would even know they're a believer. No one would think they're a passionate lover of Jesus because they're not willing to wear the holy garments. They're not willing to be different. They don't want to stand out.

But if we are willing to take on the yoke of the garments and be set apart, God will pour more of His Spirit upon us. We're going to experience more and more of the holiness, glory, and beauty of His Spirit enveloping us, clothing us, and living through us.

Jesus said to the church in Laodicea,

> Because you say, "I am rich, and have become wealthy, and have need of nothing," and you do not know that you are wretched and miserable and poor and blind and naked, I advise you to *buy* from Me gold refined by fire so that you may become rich, and *white garments* so that you may *clothe yourself*, and that the shame of your nakedness will not be revealed; and eye salve to anoint your eyes so that you may see.
>
> —Revelation 3:17–18

How do we buy these garments from the Lord? By being obedient to Him. Yeshua said, "If the world hates you, you know that it has hated Me before it hated you. If you were of the world, the world would love its own; but because you are not of the world, but I chose you out of the world, because of this the world hates you" (John 15:18–19).

As you fulfill your call to be a priest by being willing to witness for Jesus, let people know you love Him, and let your light shine before men, the power of the Holy Spirit will come upon you, clothing you with holiness, glory, and beauty.

In the next chapter, we'll take a closer look at the garments of the high priest to see what they reveal about how we are called to live as priests of God.

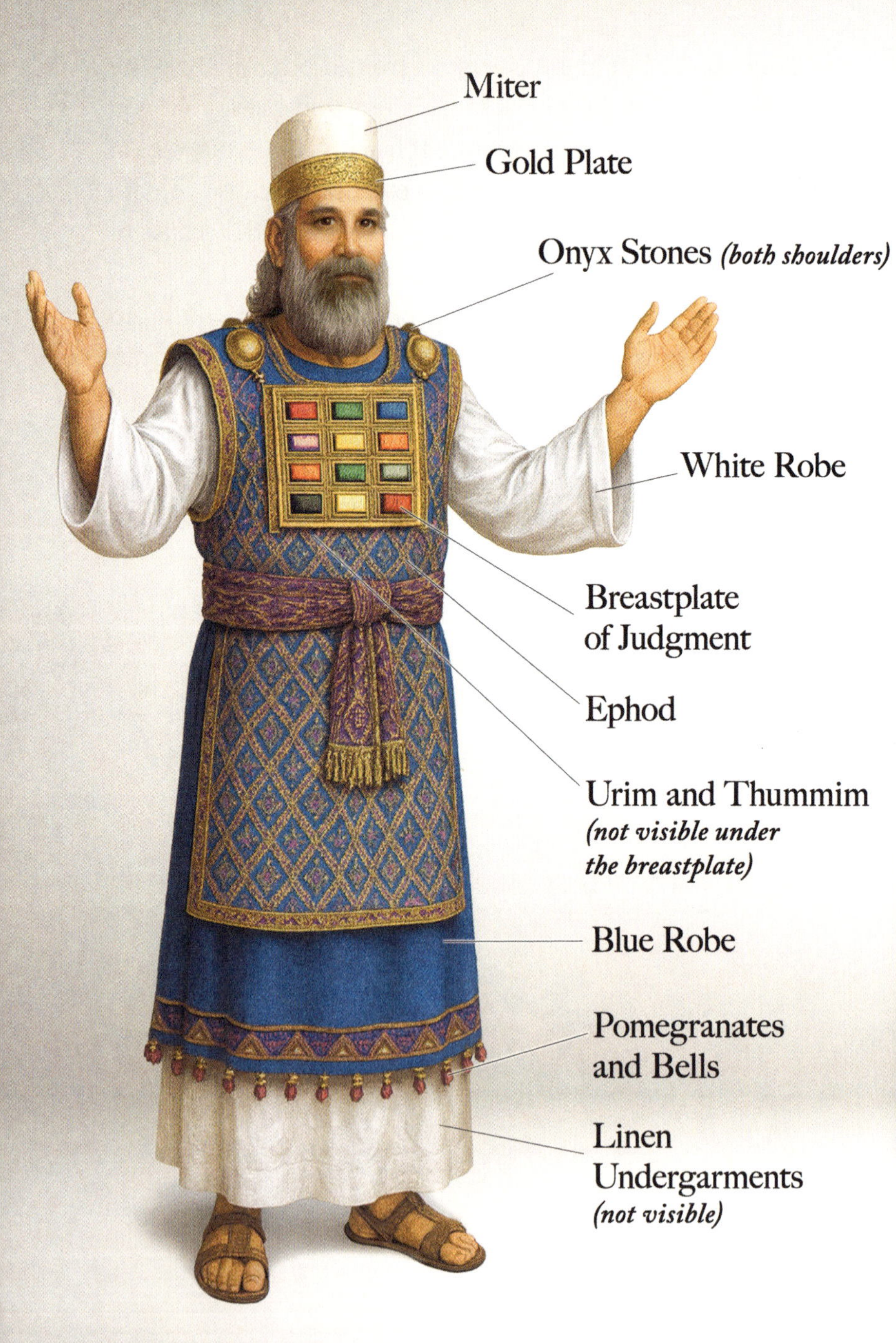

Miter
Gold Plate
Onyx Stones *(both shoulders)*
White Robe
Breastplate
of Judgment
Ephod
Urim and Thummim
*(not visible under
the breastplate)*
Blue Robe
Pomegranates
and Bells
Linen
Undergarments
(not visible)

Chapter 17

CLOTHED IN GLORY AND BEAUTY: THE HIGH PRIESTLY GARMENTS

ONCE AGAIN WE read in Exodus 28:2, "You shall make holy garments for Aaron your brother, *for glory and for beauty*." Just as the furnishings in the Tabernacle and the sacrifices offered within it are filled with prophetic meaning, so too are the garments worn by the high priest who ministered there. The Lord Himself designed each item. Every color, every detail, was spoken out of eternity and has spiritual application for our lives today.

In this final chapter, we're going to look at the garments the high priest wore and how they reveal who we are in Messiah and how we can live worthy of our calling.

THE UNDERGARMENTS

First, I'd like to point out that under his robes the high priest wore long underwear, similar to thermal long johns. Exodus 28:42 says, "You shall make for them *linen breeches to cover their bare flesh*; they shall reach from the loins even to the thighs."

Here the Lord is showing us that the flesh needs to be covered. This is critical. Many of God's people today are living in the power of the flesh and dressing to attract attention to themselves. We can't have it both ways. We can't be clothed in the spiritual garments of God's holiness, glory, and beauty and, at the same time, seek to impress others with our appearance. When we dress in a way that draws attention to our physical form, be it a woman's figure or a man's muscles, we disqualify ourselves from being conscious of the beautiful spiritual garments the Lord wants to give us.

Much of this world operates according to the power of the flesh. But James said there are two types of wisdom: wisdom from above, which is pure and heavenly, and wisdom from the earth, which is fleshly and demonic (Jas. 3:15–17). There is power in the flesh, but it is a lesser power.

I once took a tour of a company where the CEO was leading about thirty of us through the facility. As we walked, I overheard a man behind me comment to his wife, "Look how tall he is. He's a good person to be president of the company." This individual equated power with physical stature. But God's power is not from the realm of flesh.

Think about when Samuel, at the Lord's command, went to anoint one of Jesse's sons as king. Jesse lined up his sons from tallest to youngest, and Samuel went to each one thinking, "This tall, handsome man must be the one the Lord's going to anoint as king." But God kept rejecting them. Then the Lord said to Samuel, "Do not look at his appearance or at the height of his stature, because I have rejected him; for God sees not as a man sees, for man looks at the outward appearance, but the Lord looks at the heart" (1 Sam. 16:7).

We know the end of the story. God anointed little David, the shepherd boy who was playing out in the field, as king. David wasn't anointed king because he was tall or had power in the flesh. He was anointed king because he was a man after God's own heart (1 Sam. 13:14). There was something eternal inside him.

Sadly, many believers try to use their beauty, physical strength, or intellect to manipulate and intimidate people. But those who live this way never enter into the experience of wearing the heavenly garments and accessing the spiritual realities God wants to bestow on us.

God commanded the high priest to cover his flesh because He doesn't want us to be flesh-conscious. He wants us to be Spirit-conscious like Adam and Eve were until they sinned and became separated from God. If we take pleasure or find our identity in the flesh, we're living in darkness. The flesh is passing away. It will return to the dust. If Yeshua doesn't return first, everyone who is reading this book will experience the reality of their flesh decaying and dying.

We don't want to identify with what is decomposing but with the form of life that never ends. "Though our outer man is decaying, yet our inner man is being renewed day by day" (2 Cor. 4:16). This is one of the reasons Peter instructed women not to let their adornment "be merely external...but let it be the hidden person of the heart, with the imperishable quality of a gentle and quiet spirit, which is precious in the sight of God" (1 Pet. 3:3–4). It's not wrong to dress attractively and take care of ourselves to reflect God's excellence, but that shouldn't be our focus.

As I've grown in the Lord, I've even changed the way I dress. For example, I pay attention to how many buttons I leave undone on my shirt because I don't want to draw anyone to my flesh. Jude warns us to hate even the garment polluted by the flesh so we can instead receive the spiritual clothing from on high that Jesus spoke of in Luke 24:49. If you want to be clothed with garments of holiness, glory, and beauty, then you must reject the flesh.

Many people today struggle with their self-identity because the world has told them they don't measure up physically. Women think they're unattractive because they don't look like supermodels. Beautiful daughters of God walk in self-loathing because they don't measure up to the world's definition of beauty.

Men face similar battles. I'm 5'6", and it would be easy for me to be intimidated by people who are 6'2", thinking I'm less of a man because I'm shorter. But we have to reject these false identities. They are lies of fleshly, demonic origin. When we look in the mirror, we can appreciate how the Lord has made us, but we need to reject any pride concerning our appearance.

I remember once when I was ministering, looking to Jesus and praising Him, I paused and went to the restroom. When I glanced in the mirror, I heard the Holy Spirit say, "How dare you look at Me and then look at yourself." Father God wants us to keep our eyes on Jesus and receive His heavenly garments—not look at Yeshua and, at the same time, glory in our own flesh.

Not only do we need to reject the world's lies—that we're too fat, too skinny, not tall enough, not attractive enough—we also need to affirm the truth. If we've been telling ourselves that we're not attractive, not valuable, too tall, too short, too ugly—whatever it is—we have to stop agreeing with the enemy's accusations. Instead, when we look in the mirror, we can say: "I'm created in the image of God. The Father loves me. He chose me in Him. He purchased me for Himself by the blood of Yeshua. He made me a priest. I'm beautiful. God's glory is upon me. His honor is upon me. His holiness is upon me as it was on the high priest of Israel."

Beloved, clothe yourself with that truth. All flesh will pass away, but the one who does the will of God will abide forever.

The White Robe

The priest also wore a linen underrobe, or tunic.

> You shall weave the tunic of checkered work of fine linen, and shall make a turban of fine linen, and you shall make a sash, the work of a weaver.
>
> —Exodus 28:39

Though the verse doesn't say it explicitly, most scholars believe this tunic was white. In Scripture, white is a very important color. The redeemed of the Lord in heaven are clothed in white (Rev. 3:5; 7:9; 19:14), and when Jesus rose from the grave, the two angels who appeared at the tomb were in white (John 20:12). The same thing happened at Yeshua's ascension in Acts 1. Two angels dressed in white appeared. In the Book of Revelation, Jesus Himself is described as having white hair.

White is also associated with the Spirit and glory of God. Many people who have had supernatural encounters testify that the Lord manifested Himself to them in radiant white light. This is the spiritual clothing God has given us. He has clothed us with His power, His purity, His glory, and His light—all reflected in the symbolism of the white robe the high priest wore.

And here's something I love: White is not the absence of color but the fullness of it. When white light passes through a prism, it divides into all the colors of a rainbow. What does the Scripture tell us surrounds God's throne? A rainbow! (See Ezekiel 1:28; Revelation 4.) White light, then, is the perfect union of every color, and by robing us in white, God has clothed us in all the colors of the rainbow, just as He's clothed Himself.

The Blue Robe

Over the white tunic, the priest wore a blue robe. This is found in Exodus 28:31: "And you shall make the robe of the ephod all of blue."

Remember, every part of the high priest's garment was designed by God Himself. It came right out of His heart. So why did He say the high priest needed to be clothed in blue? Well, consider this: When you go outside and look up into the heavens, what color do you see on a clear day? Blue. Blue is the color of divinity. The sky is blue. The oceans are blue, and all the furniture in the Tabernacle was covered in blue (Num. 4:5–12). Consider also that the tassels, or the tzitzit, that the Lord commanded the male Israelites to wear had to have a cord of blue.

> Speak to the sons of Israel, and tell them that they shall make for themselves tassels on the corners of their garments throughout their generations, and that they shall put on the tassel of each corner a cord of blue.
>
> —Numbers 15:38

This blue robe the high priest wore points to the fact that we are citizens of heaven, and we have a heavenly calling (Phil. 3:20; Heb. 3:1).

We need to start thinking of ourselves this way—as those who have been anointed by God and clothed with heavenly robes. In fact, we've been blessed "with every spiritual blessing in the heavenly [blue] places in Christ" (Eph. 1:3).

The Pomegranates and Bells

At the bottom of the blue robe were pomegranates and bells arranged in alternating sequence.

> You shall make on its hem pomegranates of blue and purple and scarlet material, all around on its hem, and bells of gold between them all around: a golden bell and a pomegranate, a golden bell and a pomegranate, all around on the hem of the robe.
>
> —Exodus 28:33–34

Why did the Lord include bells and pomegranates? Let's start with the prophetic significance of the pomegranates.

A pomegranate is a fruit, so it points to the fruit of the Spirit. Interestingly, according to Jewish tradition, the average pomegranate has about 613 seeds. Do you know how many laws there are in the Torah, according to the sages? There are 613!

Remember too that Yeshua said, "All the laws are fulfilled in love: to love God with all our heart, strength, soul, and mind, and to love our neighbor as ourselves." (See Matthew 22:37–40.) Thus, the pomegranate represents the embodiment of the Law, which is love. I think it's no coincidence that a pomegranate is red, the color of love and of Jesus' blood.

But the blue robe's hem wasn't adorned only with pomegranates; there were also golden bells in alternating sequence. A bell makes sound. It has a voice. It gets people's attention. I believe the Lord is saying here that as you and I walk as priests before Him, we are called to proclaim the Word of God. We not only need fruit in our lives, symbolized by the pomegranate, but we also have to speak the name of Jesus. We have to witness to people and call people to Him. It's not enough just to have the fruit. People also need to hear the gospel. That's why we need the bells as well as the fruit.

Many Christians are friends with unbelievers and never tell them about Jesus. Others think their goodness is their witness. We do need to be kind and show compassion. We do need to reach out to others. But we also have to tell them about Jesus. The bells on the high priest's robe remind us that we have to speak out loud to lift up the name of Messiah Yeshua.

Yeshua said, "For whoever is ashamed of Me and *My words* in this adulterous and sinful generation, the Son of Man will also be ashamed of him when He comes in the glory of His Father with the holy angels" (Mark 8:38). This is letting us know that as priests we not only need to bear good fruit, but we also need to proclaim the good news. How are people going to believe unless somebody tells them?

Let me give you an example. Imagine I walk into a restaurant wearing my yarmulke and order a meal. My waitress has been turned off to Christianity because she grew up going to church with her parents but saw Mom and Dad live as hypocrites. Maybe her childhood pastor didn't exhibit much of the goodness and power of Jesus, so she's not convinced that Christianity is true and Jesus is the only way. As an adult she's embraced a kind of "do whatever works for you" New Age philosophy.

Then she serves my table, and she feels the fruit of the Spirit from me. She senses the warmth, peace, and love of Christ, but I never tell her about Jesus. When I leave that restaurant, I've potentially led her further away from Yeshua because she may be thinking, "He's wearing a yarmulke. Yarmulkes are for Jewish people. Jewish people don't believe in Jesus, and I felt more of God from him than I have from my parents or the other Christian people I know." Therefore, she's thinking Jewish people are closer to God than Christians. In my silence I actually lead her away from God.

But if, before I left that restaurant, I looked her in the eye and said, "I want you to know that Jesus loves you," I would have been displaying both the fruit and the bells. That's what God wants from us. The fruit and the bells are meant to work together.

In the old days, when it was time for the gospel to be preached, churches rang bells so people could come and hear the Word. Beloved, if we think we're reaching out to people in Yeshua but never tell them about Him, we're missing it. We can't just do good works. We also have to point people to the One behind those good deeds. This is our responsibility as priests. There is no other name under heaven by which men can be saved (Acts 4:12). Every one of us is called to proclaim it. All of us are called to "wear the bells." No one is exempt.

THE EPHOD

As we move on through the garments of the high priest, we come to the ephod, a colorful linen apron worn over the blue robe.

> They shall also make the ephod of gold, of blue and purple and scarlet material and fine twisted linen, the work of the skillful workman. It shall have two shoulder pieces joined to its two ends, that it may be joined.
>
> —EXODUS 28:6–7

Notice the beautiful colors of the ephod: blue, purple, gold, and scarlet. Why did the Lord specifically command that the ephod have these colors? Every detail of the priest's garments carries meaning, so what does each color symbolize?

We've already seen that blue represents the heavens. As believers in Yeshua, we have a heavenly citizenship, and we have been blessed with a holy anointing. The blue in the ephod communicates to us that we are clothed by God's Spirit with heavenly, spiritual garments.

Purple, woven into the ephod, symbolizes royalty and kingship. This is why, when the Roman soldiers crucified Jesus, they mocked Him and put on Him a purple robe as He hung on the cross with a sign above His head that said, "Jesus the Nazarene, *the king of the Jews*" (John 19:19). Scarlet, or red, speaks of the blood of Jesus and the sacrificial love of God. And the threads of gold represent the manifestation of God's glory—His *kavod*, His weight.

As a final note about the ephod, on each shoulder was an onyx stone engraved with the names of the twelve tribes of Israel—six on one side and six on the other (Exod. 28:9–10). These stones remind us that God carries His people on His shoulders. Just as He carried Israel, He carries our burdens today. Yeshua said, "Come to Me, all who are weary and heavy-laden, and I will give you rest. Take My yoke upon you and learn from Me, for I am gentle and humble in heart, and you will find rest for your souls. For My yoke is easy and My burden is light" (Matt. 11:28–30).

The Breastplate of Judgment

On the blue robe, the priest wore the breastplate of judgment, which held twelve beautiful, costly stones.

> You shall make a breastplate of judgment, the work of a skillful workman; like the work of the ephod you shall make it: of gold, of blue and purple and scarlet material and fine twisted linen you shall make it. It shall be square and folded double, a span in length and a span in width. You shall mount on it four rows of stones; the first row shall be a row of ruby, topaz and emerald; and the second row a turquoise, a sapphire and a diamond; and the third row jacinth, an agate and an amethyst; and the fourth row a beryl and an onyx and a jasper; they shall be set in gold filigree. The stones shall be according to the names of the sons of Israel….Aaron shall carry the names of the sons of Israel in the breastplate of judgment over his heart when he enters the holy place, for a memorial before the Lord continually.
>
> —Exodus 28:15–21, 29

These stones worn over the priest's heart were costly, valuable, precious stones. This communicates to us how much God loves us. I want you to hear this, beloved: To God, you are a ruby, an emerald, a sapphire, a diamond. It's like when a man gives his wife a diamond ring. He is saying to her, "You are a diamond to me." The stones on the breastplate are the costliest on earth, and this is what God uses to symbolize who we are as His people. He loves us so much that He commanded the high priest to wear these stones on the breastplate, over his heart, as a picture of how He carries us over His heart.

In Ephesians 1:18, Paul said, "I pray that the eyes of your heart may be enlightened, so that you will know what is the hope of His calling, what are the riches of the glory of His inheritance in the saints." Paul is praying that our eyes will be open so that we'll understand who we are—that we're priceless stones to Him. God has put something beautiful and precious inside us, and He wants us to see ourselves the way He sees us: deeply loved, eternally valuable, and adorned with His glory.

The Urim and Thummim

Connected to this breastplate of judgment were the mysterious Urim and Thummim stones. Exodus 28:30 says, "You shall put in the breastplate of judgment the Urim and the Thummim, and they shall be over Aaron's heart when he goes in before the Lord." The words *Urim* and *Thummim* are translated into English as "lights" and "perfection." Some have translated them as "revelation" and "truth." God gives us light, and He shows us His perfect way. He gives us revelation, and it gives us truth. We need to stop looking to the world and learn how to wait on God and trust Him. If we learn to be still, He'll teach us how to be sensitive to the voice of His Holy Spirit.

The Urim and Thummim were divine oracles that the high priest would present before the Lord when he needed to know something—and God would answer him, usually with a yes or no.

Though the Scripture speaks of them, these items are shrouded in mystery. We're not sure whetrher the Urim and Thummim were *on* the breastplate of judgment or in a pouch *under* the breastplate of judgment. But we do know that the Lord would speak to the high priest through this divine oracle.

How does this relate to us today? We are not carrying stones that help us know God's will. But we have the Holy Spirit, the Ruach HaKodesh. And when we practice cultivating the presence of God in our lives—when we discipline ourselves to sit before Him and become aware of the nuances of His Spirit within—we will be led by the Spirit. He'll tell us yes or no. He'll either give us peace about something or put a check in our hearts if it's wrong.

We don't rely on the Urim and Thummim anymore. We now rely on the Holy Spirit, who has been given to us as our indwelling inheritance.

As I've matured in the Lord, I've learned not to just run ahead in the flesh but to wait on the Lord. God has taught me a lot about knowing when He's guiding me to move forward and when He's directing me not to proceed. The Urim and Thummim are now inside us.

As we learn how to fast from the flesh, fast from relying on the world, fast from giving ourselves to the things of the world, and instead learn how to wait on the Holy Spirit, God is going to supernaturally and mystically guide us through His Ruach HaKodesh that lives inside us. The Urim and Thummin are now incarnate within us. The new mystery is Christ in you, the hope of glory (Col. 1:27).

The Miter

Last, we come to the miter, or cap. We read about this in Exodus 28:40: "You shall make caps for them, for glory and for beauty."

Everyone could see the priest's headdress, which was "for glory and for beauty," but not everyone will see the glory and beauty on you. They didn't see the glory on Jesus either. As Paul said in 1 Corinthians 2:7–8:

> We speak God's wisdom in a mystery, the hidden wisdom which God predestined before the ages to our glory; the wisdom which none of the rulers of this age has understood; for if they had understood it they would not have crucified the Lord of glory.

They plucked out His beard, spat in His face, and jeered at Yeshua when He was on the cross. But that didn't mean the glory wasn't in Him. So too the world does not see us as God sees us. As Peter the apostle said, we are rejected by men but precious in the sight of God (1 Pet. 2:4).

You might not always feel like you have glory, but the world doesn't define who you are, just as the world didn't define who Yeshua was. No matter how you're treated by the world, you're a costly ruby, a sapphire, an emerald, a diamond to God. The riches of His glory are in you. You're crowned as a priest of the Lord with glory and beauty. Look to Yahweh alone for your identity. Lift up your head!

We also read that over the priest's forehead was a gold plate that said, "Holy to the LORD."

> You shall also make a plate of pure gold and shall engrave on it, like the engravings of a seal, "Holy to the LORD." You shall fasten it on a blue cord, and it shall be on the turban; it shall be at the front of the turban. It shall be on Aaron's forehead, and Aaron shall take away the iniquity of the holy things which the sons of Israel consecrate, with regard to all their holy gifts; and it shall always be on his forehead, that they may be accepted before the LORD.
>
> —EXODUS 28:36–38

That's who you and I are—holy to the Lord! The Bible says we're a holy nation and a royal priesthood (1 Pet. 2:9). We are set apart to God. Just as this proclamation was always over the priest's head, we need to internalize the fact that we are holy. We belong to God. We are holy because we belong to Him.

If you had a condemning parent growing up, don't let that be the band around your head. If you were bullied and rejected, don't let those words of hate be the voice over your head. If you've had self-image problems, cast those voices off because that's not what God wants above your head. His gold plate is over your head, declaring that you are His. You are

His possession—bought by the blood of Yeshua, sealed by the Holy Spirit, set apart, and sanctified by His Word. You are holy. This is your new identity in Christ.

You're gold to Him. May you always remember that.

Conclusion

THE MYSTERY REVEALED

As we come to the end of this journey through the Tabernacle, let's take a moment to reflect on what we've seen. From the very first step into the Outer Court to the garments worn by the high priest, every detail of the Mishkan has pointed us to Messiah Yeshua and reveals God's desire to draw us close.

We began by looking at the Gate, the only way in. Just as there was only one entrance into the Tabernacle, so too Yeshua is the one way into the presence of God. From there we came to the Brazen Altar, where the blood was shed. This pointed us to the cross, where our sins were judged in Messiah once and for all. Then we saw the Brass Laver, where the priests washed daily. In this we learned that even though our sins have been forgiven, we still need the ongoing cleansing of the Holy Spirit in our lives.

As we entered the Holy Place, we encountered the Golden Menorah—the light of the Spirit. We cannot walk with God without being led by the Ruach HaKodesh. Then came the Table of Showbread, revealing Father's love for us and His desire to feed us with His very presence. From there we came to the Altar of Incense, which speaks of perpetual prayer and worship rising before the throne.

Then we arrived at the Veil, the great barrier that once separated humanity from God's presence. Yet when Yeshua died, the Veil was torn from top to bottom. Today, the way into the Holy of Holies is open to us, and we can come boldly before the throne of grace. There in the Holy of Holies was the Ark of the Covenant, along with Aaron's rod that budded, the jar of manna, and two tablets with the Ten Commandments. Each item reveals something of God's nature and His relationship with us: Aaron's rod reminds us to honor and submit to God-ordained authority, the jar of manna points to God's supernatural provision, and the Ten Commandments reveal His character and loving protection.

Above the Ark was the Mercy Seat, where the high priest poured out the blood of the sacrifice once a year on Yom Kippur to atone for the sins of Israel. There, between the two cherubim, is where the glory of God dwelled. In Messiah Jesus, this is where you and I are invited to abide—in the very presence of God.

We also studied the sacrifices: the burnt offering, the grain offering, the peace offering, and the sin and trespass offerings. And we saw how each one pointed to Yeshua's once-for-all sacrifice and our response of worship, thanksgiving, surrender, and repentance. Then we examined the garments of the high priest, with each item revealing not only how we are to live as priests of God today but who we are in Messiah Jesus—holy, chosen, and loved.

Beloved, the Tabernacle is more than history. It is God's prophetic blueprint for intimacy with Him. From the Outer Court to the Holy of Holies, the Tabernacle reveals His heart to draw near to us and be our God.

Through Yeshua, God no longer dwells in a tent made with hands. He dwells in us. We are His tabernacle, His temple, His priests, His dwelling place. He holds us close to His heart, covers us with garments of glory and beauty, and calls us to shine His light in this dark world.

As we close this book, I pray we will open our hearts even wider to the One who longs to fill them. May His Spirit dwell richly within us. And may we become living tabernacles where the world can encounter the love and power of God.

A PERSONAL INVITATION FROM THE AUTHOR

God loves you deeply. His Word is filled with promises that reveal His desire to bring healing, hope, and abundant life to every area of your being—body, mind, and spirit. More than anything, He wants a personal relationship with you through His Son, Jesus Christ.

If you've never invited Jesus into your life, you can do so right now. It's not about religion; it's about a relationship with the One who knows you completely and loves you unconditionally. If you're ready to take that step, simply pray this prayer with a sincere heart:

> *Lord Jesus, I want to know You as my Savior and Lord. I confess and believe that You are the Son of God and that You died for my sins. I believe that You rose from the dead and are alive today. Please forgive me for my sins. I invite You into my heart and my life. Make me new. Help me walk with You, grow in Your love, and live for You every day. In Jesus' name, amen.*

To hear a personal message from me about following Yeshua, scan this QR code or visit RabbiSchneiderBooks.com/tabernacle/resources.

If you just prayed that prayer, you've made the most important decision of your life. All of heaven rejoices with you, and so do I! You are now a child of God, and your journey with Him has just begun. Please reach out to my publisher at pray4me@charismamedia.com if you accepted Jesus today or if this book has encouraged or impacted your life in any way. We'd love to celebrate with you and send you free materials to help strengthen your faith. We look forward to hearing from you!

Dear beloved one,

If you enjoyed this book and believe others would benefit from reading it, please leave a review on Amazon and recommend it to others, because there is a great need for this teaching among God's people.

Wishing you God's best,

Rabbi Schneider

www.DiscoveringTheJewishJesus.com

 /Discovering the Jewish Jesus with Rabbi Schneider

 facebook.com/rabbischneider

 @RabbiSchneider

Roku—Discovering the Jewish Jesus

Apple TV—Discovering the Jewish Jesus

Amazon App—Discovering the Jewish Jesus

 Podcast—Discovering the Jewish Jesus

Search for Rabbi Schneider and Discovering the Jewish Jesus on your favorite platform.

For a complete list of Rabbi Schneider's television and radio broadcasts, visit www.DiscoveringTheJewishJesus.com.